When the Sun Goes Down *is practical, fun, and thought provoking. Reading through it sparks one's creativity and a sense of play in an area that has been shrouded in darkness for too long!*

Christiane Northrup, M. D.
Author of *Mother-Daughter Wisdom*

The problem addressed in Betty Breuhaus's practical and amusing book is: If you don't plan your own funeral, someone else will. It's hard to write breezily about such a dark topic, but When the Sun Goes Down *succeeds, marvelously. There is useful information—you CAN avoid singing "Amazing Grace," if you wish—valuable tips, and a tone of informed serendipity that make this book a pleasure to read.*

I wasn't looking forward to my funeral before reading this book . . . Well, I'm still not, but now the pill may be a bit easier to swallow.

Alex Beam, *Boston Globe* columnist

When the Sun Goes Down *is about how to truly celebrate a life well lived. It is hard to imagine how a book about funeral planning can be so much fun to read. But this book is! It is a heartfelt and informative guide that covers the details of end-of-life planning and is interspersed with wisdom, humor, and zest. It is the perfect book for every book club to read and discuss. It is guaranteed to spark wonderful, meaningful conversations with family and friends. No one should wait till the end of his or her life to reflect on what matters. Laugh, learn, and plan your way through this book. Reading it is a gift to yourself and to the people you care about.*

Paula K. Rauch, M.D.
Director, MGH Cancer Center Parenting Program:
Parenting At a Challenging Time
Massachusetts General Hospital
Harvard Medical School

Ms. Breuhaus presents us with a book ostensibly about death, but actually about life; a book dealing with grief, that dares seek joy.

It's a quirky, brave, often funny work, infused with the bracing air of independent thought.

Francis T. Mayo, Estate Attorney

I didn't know what to expect when I picked up When the Sun Goes Down, *but immediately was enthralled in a thoughtful and personal discussion of life, death, and funerals. This book is a valuable resource to stimulate people's thinking about what they want their funeral to be like. A personal celebration and farewell that would epitomize your life, loves, and personality is what most of us desire. Betty Breuhaus shows us how to achieve that goal by preplanning, imagining broad possibilities, and not leaving details to chance. This is a must read at any age, whether you are young or old. How do you want to be remembered? Beginning with the end in mind is a useful way to think of your life and your last hurrah.*

Judy Waterston, President
Spaulding Rehabilitation Hospital

Betty Breuhaus has presented a difficult subject in an interesting and positive manner. In our lives, we plan many events with our family. Here she provides a guide to help the reader plan their final celebration, their funeral.

Read this guide, involve your family and consult with your funeral director to plan an event which will reflect your own personal style and, most importantly, help your survivors grieve and celebrate you.

Murphy Family
Murphy Funeral Home

No one's going to the grave with their music still inside them if Betty Breuhaus has her way.

Her gutsy new book, When the Sun Goes Down: Planning the Funeral of Your Life, *cracks open the greatest secret in the world; the process of arranging your own innovative funeral now, opens the potential to accept your own mortality, and in so doing, creates the potential to live free from fear.*

When my beloved father-in-law Corbett Monica died, 300 stand-up comedians and friends came to say good-bye to one of their own. Each took a turn at the microphone, doing bits of their own act, and some blatantly stealing parts of his act. As we laughed and cried our way through our goodbyes, we all knew he would not have wanted it any other way.

Real personalized funerals not only "look" different than traditional funerals, they "feel" different. The difference is the emotional content. A real personalized funeral is an experience that delivers a powerful personal insight and a powerful emotional connection. It leaves survivors with a strong and lasting sense of who you were to them. It leaves participants with a living and sustainable memory of you that will never die. This is no small gift to give. When accomplished, its effect is felt forever.

If you think you are ready to face one of the most rewarding tasks of your lifetime, let Betty Breuhaus guide you through the development of your own funeral.

It's a must-read for everyone, funeral directors and their advanced need planners included.

Bill Bates, President
Life Appreciation Seminars

WHEN THE SUN GOES DOWN:
Planning the Funeral of Your Life

WHEN THE SUN GOES DOWN:
Planning the Funeral of Your Life

Includes a Personal Funeral Planner
and
A Guide for Book Club Discussions

Betty Breuhaus

PublishingWorks, Inc.
Exeter, NH
2008

PublishingWorks, Inc.
60 Winter Street
Exeter, NH 03833
603-778-9883
For Sales and Orders:
1-800-738-6603 or 603-772-7200

Cover photo by Kat Mack,
        courtesy of Exeter Monuments.
Author Photo by Bryan Burns

Designed by: Kat Mack
LCCN: 2008925151
ISBN: 1-933002-76-X
ISBN-13: 978-1-933002-76-7

To

Bill

Katie

and the best friends anyone could ever have

AUTHOR'S NOTE

Although the word "funeral" is generally used to describe a rite held to mark death with a body present, I have used the word in a broader sense. In my definition, I have included any service, with or without a body present.

The anecdotes found throughout the book are meant to support and clarify the text. While they are all based on true-life experiences, I have taken some liberties in relating them.

WHEN THE SUN GOES DOWN
… it is rising somewhere else. And so goes the cycle of life.

I am standing upon the seashore
A ship at my side spreads her white
sails to the morning breeze and starts
for the blue ocean.

She is an object of beauty and strength.
I stand and watch her until at length
she hangs like a speck of white cloud
just where the sea and sky come
to mingle with each other.

Then, someone at my side says;
"There, she is gone!"

"Gone where?"
Gone from my sight. That is all.
She is just as large in mast and hull
and spar as she was when she left my side
and she is just as able to bear her
load of living freight to her destined port.
Her diminished size is in me, not in her.

And just at the moment when someone
at my side says, "There, she is gone!"
There are other eyes watching her coming,
and other voices ready to take up the glad
shout;
"Here she comes!"
And that is dying.

—Henry van Dyke

Acknowledgments

For their tireless and patient editing of this book, I must thank Katie Kaseler, Susan Bridges, Carol Lacoss, Ran Niehoff, Paula Rauch, Brian Breuhaus, and my most nonjudgmental editor, Apple Spell-check. Tombstone drawings were created by Tam Cronin. Many thanks to my husband, Bill Darling, for listening tirelessly to my yearlong observations on death.

And perhaps most important, I am extremely indebted to my two constant companions in the office: my golden retriever, Martha May; and my six-foot-tall, life-sized cardboard figure of Red Sox slugger David Ortiz.

FOREWORD

When the Sun Goes Down offers insightful advice and serves as a handbook for all those who want to take responsibility for the final chapter of their personal lives. This helpful book begins with a focus on planning one's own funeral or memorial celebration but ends up delivering useful tools and warm encouragement to begin experiencing a fuller, happier life today!

Written like the plot of a gripping story, this book actually provides a step-by-step journey for the reader. A creative, energetic, successful businesswoman, wife, and mother, Betty has done her homework and visited the subject thoroughly. It's as if she has created a "Let's Go ..." guidebook with practical itineraries for thoughtful travelers in this field. And along the way, her narrative sparkles with humor, the anecdotes delight, and the profound quotations she has gathered are, by themselves, worth the price of the book. The French existentialist, Albert Camus, totally absorbed with making the most of the meaning of being a person, taught that "those who do not come to terms with death are unable to fully experience life." Read this book—enjoy it—it will help you reaffirm the gift of life!

> Dr. Randall H. Niehoff
> Sr. Minister,
> Sanibel Congregational
> United Church of Christ

INTRODUCTION

Plan your own funeral? Perhaps eating aged sushi or being barraged with high definition techno tunes seem like more attractive alternatives. Why in the world would you do that? You're not dying. Well, I've got news. No matter how rich you are, how smart you are, or how powerful you are, no one gets out of this world alive. Even he who dies with the most toys is still dead. Maybe it's time to get off that comfortable couch of denial. Now is the time to put together that inevitable final celebration of your life—your funeral. Take charge and put together a plan that is so innovative and personal that everyone who attends will feel your very presence and go away inspired to live a more worthwhile life. And while creating this plan, you may find that you have the added benefit of a fresh perspective on your life right now!

Numerous books have been written with standard forms to be filled out and specific instructions to be followed for planning your funeral. *When the Sun Goes Down* makes a giant leap of faith and suggests that you create your very own funeral service. Just as traditional wedding vows did not quite "say it all" at your wedding, nor did the traditional "hospital birth" suffice for your baby's delivery, you need not compromise this final celebration of your life with a customary funeral service. You are entitled to make this last celebration of your life entirely your own. The information in this book is meant to spark your imagination and assist you in this exciting and stimulating process.

Traditional funerals are currently going the way of rotary telephones. Many people are even choosing to forgo funerals on the mistaken assumption that they are unnecessary. The idea that "Everyone is suffering enough without all the added confusion" is a terrible misconception since dealing with grief in a healthy manner is vital. A funeral is an important part of this process. A funeral is about the person who has died, but it is really for the living. Your loved ones need to gather together to share their memories and support each other in their grief. They need to cry, laugh, hug, and remember together. A funeral is a time for the significance of your life to be celebrated. So why not be the author of this celebration?

A common misconception is that a funeral is inescapably coupled with a church and clergy. Although this is traditionally the case, it is not compulsory. You are free to personally define exactly the type and style of life celebration you prefer. Spiritual services may be held within the church walls or outdoors in a garden. More secular services can have tremendous power. Personalize this service and make it your own.

Funerals are often of the cookie-cutter variety. While in emotional turmoil, loved ones call a funeral home, and the details of the service proceed at a rapid and uncontrolled pace. You are given choices, but they are limited and must be made immediately. A wake with an open casket? The deceased dressed in a coat and tie, which is so foreign to him that he is unrecognizable? Everyone gathered in a stuffy little room at the back of the funeral parlor? Canned music? Profuse flowers giving off a sweet and heavy odor? And then a service the next day in a church the departed would have rather died than attend. Leading the service is a clergy person who never laid eyes on the deceased and has to sneak a look at his note cards to reference the name. This is followed by a graveside ceremony with a $4,000 casket being lowered into the ground with no one watching.

Then, a reception either at the church or in a dreary function hall. People roam the room uncomfortably, sipping sweet punch and nibbling sandpaper cookies, "comforting" the grieving with such phrases as "He's in a better place now," or perhaps "We'll miss him." Tears are avoided, and eyes are averted. The guests leave thinking the survivors are "so strong."

There are many alternatives to this rather maudlin scenario. Now is the time to creatively plan the final celebration of your life. We seem to find plenty of time to anticipate and plan other milestones in life: weddings, birthdays, and retirement parties are all given lots of thought and preparation. However, the events surrounding a death are certainly not conducive to the same feelings or time frame. The loss of a loved one is a time of stress and grief, regardless of the situation. Often, the pressure of planning a funeral puts so much strain on the survivors that they fight among themselves. Each knew you "best" and "knows" what you would have wanted. So, to present your loved ones with plans to mark this final event is one of the greatest gifts you can give.

Your funeral service should be a reflection of who you were, the people you loved, what you believed in, what you accomplished, and what you did for fun. Did you marry a wonderful woman and share fifty years with her? Tell us what that meant to you. Did you raise wonderful children and now have fabulous grandchildren? Tell us how that affected you. Did you volunteer your time and give something back to the community? Tell us how that changed you. What are you most proud of? What was your greatest disappointment? What made you laugh? Did you work to protect the environment? Did you create a garden? Did you golf every conceivable moment you could? Did you know every Red Sox player on the roster? Did you swim every day? Did you have the coolest car on the block? Did you carve wooden eagles? Did you paint? Did you read? Did you write? Reviewing your interests and your values will give you a fresh perspective. And it will give your loved ones a much deeper understanding of you and what made you tick. This funeral will be yours!

Planning your funeral also sets a budget. If you define what you want, no one will have a problem with their conscience later. They will know that you want a plain pine casket and not the 18-gauge orchid-brushed casket with pink velvet interior. They will know your wishes concerning the disposition of your body and will not have to make that very personal decision for you. Nor will they have to guess about the gathering afterward. What would you most like? A formal reception or a picnic in the woods? Champagne and foie gras, beer and sausages, or iced tea and animal crackers? At such a stressful time, articulating your desires makes everyone more comfortable and keeps costs real without imagined pressure.

Your funeral should be so full of your spirit that your very presence is felt. This service is your final chance to share your life philosophies. People whose lives you have touched will be gathered together. Organizing this service will demonstrate that your caring for them transcends death. Now is the time to pass on worthy lessons and wisdom you have garnered during your lifetime.

Ideally, people will leave this event not only having felt your essence, but also with a new perspective on life and how to live it more fully and meaningfully. The ideal funeral will teach the attendees something about living. What a wonderful way to celebrate your life.

Planning your funeral may also have an immediate personal benefit for you. People's attitudes toward death have long been an indication of how they lived. Thinking about death puts a perspective on living. You may gain fresh insights about how you are currently living, which can change your actions and attitudes right now. Americans, in particular, tend to ignore death and not embrace it as a part of life. This attitude can skew both short- and long-term decisions. Sensing that life is finite challenges procrastination. Do you want to see the coast of Alaska? Go! This perspective might also foster forgiveness and reconciliation. Was that past snub really so cruel and unforgivable? Do you have time to live with it any longer? Come on … let it go.

So go to it! Open your heart and mind to one of life's inescapable sure things. Have the final say. Define your own dignity. Have some fun with it. Take the time to thank and acknowledge the people in your life who have been meaningful. By planning thoughtfully and creatively, you will be giving an invaluable gift to all your loved ones, and you may even change your life in the process.

Death is more universal than life; everyone dies but not everyone lives.

   —A. Sachs (1935–), justice, South African
    Constitutional Court

Under the sod and
under the trees,
Lies the body of
JONATHON PEASE
He is not here, there's only
the pod
Pease shelled out and went
to God

–

Nantucket, Massachusetts

I.

BENEFITS OF A FUNERAL

*Give sorrow words. The grief that does not speak whispers the
o'erfraught heart and bids it break.*
　　　　　—Shakespeare (1564–1616), Macbeth

GRIEF

Omitting a funeral at your death is like removing the
spark plug from an engine. Grief is a natural and universal
process after a death. Funerals provide the structure to begin
a healthy grieving process. If you choose to just quietly have
your body disposed of, have no service, and have everyone
continue on with their lives seemingly untouched by your
death, you might believe it will be easier on your family.
Though it might be "easier" in terms of less work, a funeral
affords a healthier first step in your loved ones' journey
through grief.

Physicians have referred to grief as a hidden illness. A funeral
provides a time to grieve and to receive support from friends
and family. To deny the pain does not make it disappear, but
merely postpones it. The American traditions of sanitizing and
avoiding the realities of death are great fodder for therapists
who must help people through their unresolved issues with
grief years later. Denial of pain can cause social disorders such
as drug or alcohol abuse, as well as other physical maladies.
Although grief and tears might appear gauche or "out of
control," they are healthy and validate loss. Grief is not the
enemy, but rather a healthy and natural process.

Funerals allow people a time period to be together, to cry,
to hug one another, and to share the loss. A widower needs
to be allowed to talk … and talk and talk and talk. A funeral
gives people a structure for both offering and accepting
comfort, a structure for healthy grief.

When Barbara's husband died, he had arranged to have no funeral. He didn't want to make it harder on his wife, family, and friends. Barbara had none of the benefits of a funeral and never really accepted his death. She did not move through the progression of healthy grief and still cried at the mention of his name until the day she died.

Weeping is perhaps the most human and universal of all relief measures.
—Dr. Karl Menninger (1893–1990),
U.S. Psychiatrist

DENIAL

Where belief is painful, we are slow to believe.
—Ovid (43 B.C.–A.D. 17)

The first stage of grief is denial. It can seem not only inconceivable that one will never see a loved one again, but utterly overwhelming as well. Denial is a form of emotional shock. However, resolving denial is a necessary ingredient in the grieving process. A funeral confirms the reality of a death.

The decision to view the body of the deceased is, of course, a personal choice. Varied situations dictate different decisions. If a person has had a prolonged illness, it can be a real comfort for their loved ones to see them finally at peace. Others prefer to remember the person as they were at their most vibrant. However, increasingly professionals deem it therapeutic for at least those closest to the deceased to view the body. Facing this reality may seem harsh when people are already in pain, but people need reality and closure. Though seemingly illogical, this exposure might well initiate "good grief."

Anna's grief when her six-year-old daughter was struck and killed by an automobile seemed bottomless. When Anna arrived at the hospital, her precious Cynthia already was dead. Doctors, and even her minister, tried to keep her from viewing the body. Because she was so insistent, they finally relented. Later she recounted the comfort it had given her, as she had imagined it to be so much worse. Reality reins in the imagination.

ESTABLISHING THE SIGNIFICANCE OF THE LOSS

And ever has it been that love knows not its own depth until the hour of separation.
> —Kahlil Gibran (1883–1931), Lebanese artist
> and poet

A funeral establishes two forms of significance. On the one hand, a service defines the loss suffered by the loved ones left behind. When something exciting happens to you, you have a bursting need to tell others. Significance of any event is crucial, be it good or bad. A widow needs to be allowed to talk about her pain and what her husband's death means to her. Listening might not be comfortable for others, but it is vital for her. Second, the social significance is established. Your family and friends need to know how much you meant to others. For them to know that others also feel a loss is reassuring.

Your loved ones will only truly understand the significance your death has on them after you are gone. A time will come when they want to tell you something, and you are not there. A time when they need comfort, and you are not there. If the significance of a loss is not established, the event can become an obsession. Conceivably, twenty years later, a woman might remain fixated on her husband's death, still trying to explain what the loss meant to her. People must be sure that others

CELEBRITY
EPITAPHS

THAT'S ALL
FOLKS!
-
MEL BLANC

understand their loss. A good funeral gives people a platform to remember and talk about the departed, to clarify their loss.

You may think that if you don't talk about a loss, people won't think about it. Wrong. They will, regardless of your conversations with them. They need to talk about their loss. And your sympathy does not make them feel worse. On the contrary, if your sympathy is real, based on understanding, it is a great comfort. It should be noted that it is sympathy, not empathy, that is called for in these situations. Try not to compare a loss you have had to another's loss. People are full of their own pain and do not want to have a grief competition. It is imperative that grief not be trivialized. The attempt to "cheer someone up" during this initial grieving process is a big mistake. Grief is not the enemy. Grief should be recognized as natural and healthy.

A funeral also defines the significance the deceased had to the community. The meaning of a person's life may be defined by the memories he or she leaves behind in others. The presence of all the people who take the time to attend a funeral, literally "paying respect," is a wonderful tribute. The worth and significance of the person is clearly in evidence.

When Carol looked around the room and saw all the people who had come to attend her mother's funeral, her spirit lifted. Family, friends from work, old school chums, neighborhood friends, and church friends were all congregated together. The worth of her mother's life was right there for Carol to see and feel.

TRANSITIONAL TIME

Death ends a life, not a relationship.
> —Morrie Schwartz (1916–1995),
>
> American educator

Your funeral is also an important time of transition. A death is not the end of a relationship, but a redefinition of it. You are gone, and your loved ones are left to establish a new relationship with you. For, although you are physically gone, your spirit lives on in all these people. They will think of you often. Your presence is now felt through memories. And when they are making decisions that you might have been a part of previously, your input will still be felt. Now your physical being is gone, but your influence is not. The funeral and gathering afterward are an integral part of this transition.

> **Odd Deaths**
>
> ISADORA
> DUNCAN
> Actress
> 1927
> She accidentally
> strangled when
> her scarf
> caught in a car
> wheel

A minister was counseling a man whose closest friend, Chuck, had just died. The grief-stricken man was listening respectfully when he suddenly blurted out, "But WHERE is Chuck right now?"

The minister sighed and said, "Were you ever really inside Chuck's skin to know where he was?"

"Well no," was the reply.

"Then he is right where he has always been for you. He is in your heart. That hasn't changed."

STRUCTURE

The very structure of the funeral is helpful to people at a time when their lives are in upheaval. A death disrupts routines for everyone and can leave periods of seemingly endless time. This time period is one of the final opportunities for the survivors to "do something" for their lost loved one. A funeral provides meaningful and defined activities for people to carry out at a time when self-directed actions are quite difficult. Ideally, people work together within the constructs of a funeral.

> When Becky and Julia's father died, there were many details that needed to be addressed. There were rooms to be reserved for out of town people, food to be prepared, and countless errands to be run. As they bounced from one task to another, they had a sense of purpose. Each felt that they were actually doing something for their father. The activity was comforting.

Enough said—it is very, very important to your family and friends that you have a funeral. So while you're at it, why not make it a great funeral, a personal funeral that will help them remember you well.

Wesley Music, in Great Britain, has launched a service to allow distant mourners to watch funerals live online. Funeral homes make a one-time payment for access to a funeral web cast. A small camera is mounted at the service, and mourners are given a password to access the event.

HENRY EDSEL SMITH
Looked up the elevator shaft
to see if the car was on the
way down
... it was

–

Albany, New York

TO DIE,

IS BUT TO LIVE

FOREVER

Jonathon Mooers
Nantucket, Massachusetts

Here lies an ATHEIST
All dressed up
And no place to go

–

Thurmont, Maryland

II.

FUNERAL HOMES

Funeral homes can be as disparate in style as Jackson Pollack and Monet. Selecting a funeral home is a key ingredient in the planning process. It is very likely that a funeral home will be involved in at least some aspect of your funeral, although this involvement varies radically. Ordinarily, a funeral home handles at the very least the disposition of the body, the death certificate, and other legal documents. On the other hand, a funeral home can handle every detail, from caring for the loved ones at the deceased's side to arranging for transportation to the airport at the funeral's end.

Funeral costs vary widely. Costs may start at $500 and easily go to more than $10,000. Decide what role you want the funeral home to play. One of the most important services a funeral home can provide is support for your survivors. Funeral directors offer knowledgeable, emotional support in all kinds of situations. Directors have been through the process countless times and may well have suggestions for circumstances that you would be hard-pressed to anticipate. The loss of a loved one is an incredibly emotional time for the survivors. If you have confidence in the funeral director, you will feel reassured, knowing that your family will be dealt with kindly at this difficult time.

Funeral homes can also offer invaluable help in dealing with children. They have materials for talking to children about death and the funeral experience. The sooner a child gains a healthy perspective on the realities of death and its part in life, the better. Make this experience as positive as is appropriate. The knowledge a funeral home has to offer can be quite supportive.

Another aspect to consider when making prearrangements for your funeral is that plans made through funeral homes are legally binding and must be carried out. If you discuss different plans with family and friends, they will not have the authority to override the arrangements you previously made with a funeral home.

FUNERAL HOME PERSONALITIES

Tom Ton was a famous circus performer from the early 1900s in the sideshow, "The Fat Man." Weighing 1,600 pounds, his casket had to be custom made extra wide and sturdy with 12 handles. It wouldn't even fit through the funeral home's doors. The casket weighed 200 pounds itself, and was the size of a small fishing boat. It took 16 pall bearers to carry his casket.

Although funeral homes all look quite similar from the outside, each has its own distinct personality. One may be quite grand and elegant, while another is more simple and cozy. Ask friends and acquaintances for recommendations to learn what your community has to offer.

A funeral director is not necessarily kind and helpful any more than a doctor is always wise and compassionate. Meet with the personnel at various funeral homes to get to know them. Increasingly, people are choosing the avocation of funeral director later in life. Men and women who have had life experiences with funerals, both good and bad, want to be a part of this process and help others at a difficult time. There is also merit in the smaller, privately owned funeral homes. Oftentimes these businesses have been owned and run by the same family for generations, and their personnel are local and active in their communities. It is best to interview more than one funeral director and get a feel for their personalities and accommodations. Whether its involvement is minimal or all-inclusive, the funeral home plays a pivotal part in your funeral planning process.

You will be working closely with these people in all aspects of your planning. If you want the type of funeral that would incorporate a brass band leading the way to the cemetery—a New Orleans Jazz Funeral—make sure the funeral directors are not "silent prayer" people.

ALL-INCLUSIVE PACKAGES

Funeral packages can be thoroughly inclusive, offering such services as helping to notify family and friends, picking up people at the airport, making accommodation plans, providing funeral transportation, coordinating with clergy, arranging flowers, organizing luncheons or gatherings before or after the service, and even offering legal advice when appropriate. The funeral director may also plan and deliver the actual funeral service. Again, the funeral home's scope of involvement is your personal choice.

Another option is to not only pre-plan your funeral, but to pay for it in advance as well. One advantage to this is that you are locked into the current rates. And, of course, it greatly simplifies everything for your loved ones. However, there are a few considerations to bear in mind. The selected funeral home must still be reputable as well as stable and in business when your time comes. There are also differences in how wisely your prepayment is invested. And, in this mobile society, the location of the funeral home must remain convenient for your friends and family.

CELEBRITY
EPITAPHS

CALLED
BACK

-

EMILY
DICKINSON
(SELF WRITTEN)

À LA CARTE

You may also choose to order à la carte from funeral homes. A federal regulation, the Funeral Rule of 1982, requires that funeral homes price each of their goods and services separately so that you know exactly what you are paying for.

Goods sold usually include caskets, urns, and various mementos. Certainly many, if not all, of these goods may be purchased elsewhere. Recently, funeral homes have been unfairly criticized about their pricing, but a good funeral home will have caskets and urns at varying costs with a wide range of options. The convenience factor should not be overlooked. If the casket is purchased directly from the funeral home, there is much less chance of its not being delivered on time or of it being defective.

Services vary widely and may be selected individually as well. Go through the funeral home's itemized lists of services and determine which are for you. Making your wishes known now eliminates the potentially guilt-driven, emotional decisions that might be made otherwise.

Some funeral homes are quite helpful with creative options. The Busch Funeral Home in Cleveland, Ohio, for example, has quite a diversity of choices in many areas. There are more than fifty choices for locations around the city to hold services. This funeral home also offers the release of butterflies, balloons, or doves at the conclusion of the service. The personalization choices are almost endless.

LIFE APPRECIATION

Another question to ask a funeral home is whether or not it has participated in the Life Appreciation course given nationwide by Bill Bates, a pioneer in developing personalized services through funeral homes. His course helps funeral directors to understand that the service should be personal and reflect the personality of the deceased. The Life Appreciation course is powerful and can be instrumental in training funeral directors to listen and help you create a more beautiful and meaningful service. If you can find someone who has trained with Bill Bates, you know your service will likely be handled your way. Choose the funeral home that is right for you.

Frank and his father Frank Sr. set out to find a funeral home that was just right. It was not unlike the choices that faced Goldielocks. The first home was paneled in a dark wood veneer, with a maroon shag carpet, and a small dimly lit entrance with artificial flowers. Too somber, they agreed. Next they encountered a brightly-lit room with small pink roses stenciled all around the ceiling. The plastic chairs screeched as they were pulled across the linoleum floor. Marginal as well, they decided. Finally they came upon a lovely old building, with a dignified entryway leading into a room carpeted with a beautiful oriental rug, and surrounded by heavy brass lighting fixtures. Just right, they concurred!

FUNERAL HOME ALTERNATIVES

Cemeteries, crematories, and casket stores are beginning to arrange entire funerals. Choosing one of these alternatives does not necessarily simplify the process, as there are certain basic issues that must be dealt with regardless of who is making the arrangements. Be aware that businesses other than funeral homes are not bound by the same regulations as licensed funeral homes. It would therefore be wise to investigate these businesses quite extensively.

As you move along through this book, you will be presented with ideas for many interesting and creative alternatives to funeral homes.

THE BEST IS YET TO COME

Francis Albert Sinatra

EZEKIAL AIKLE
Here lies Ezekial Aikle
Age 102
The Good Die Young

–

East Dalhousie, Nova Scotia

III.

DISPOSITION OF THE BODY

Now ... what to do with this container you have been living in all these years. One of the most personal decisions you must make is what to do with your body after death. This choice is the single most important information to leave in writing to your survivors.

There are two fundamental choices: burial or cremation. Certain religions, such as Orthodox Judaism and Islam, strictly forbid cremation. Most often, however, the disposition of the body is a personal choice.

Both ground burial and cremation advocates claim environmental superiority. Crematories are criticized for admitting harmful pollutants into the air, and ground burial advocates are accused of allowing hazardous chemicals from the embalming process into the ground. Pick your poison.

BURIAL

I could never be buried with people to whom I had not been introduced.
> —Norman Parkinson (1913–1990),
> celebrated English portrait and fashion
> photographer

The next choice is to decide where you want to be buried. If you decide to be buried in a cemetery, you can choose to be buried underground of aboveground in a mausoleum. Next is the question of the location of the burial plot or interment crypt. Bear in mind that this decision may affect your survivors more than you think. Both the view from this site and your neighbors are important. Your loved ones may well prefer a pleasant vista while "visiting" you. And there is always the possibility that they might not want to share this space with a local family who has always been cantankerous.

Different cemeteries have different requirements for what they call "burial vaults." These outer containers hold the original casket and keep the ground from collapsing over time. The prices and regulations for these vary greatly. Some are so tightly sealed that a flood can leave them floating above ground. Nothing is going to preserve a body or casket forever. Thus, there are numerous considerations to be addressed.

Unique Burials

In April of 2007, a wealthy farmer in southern India was granted his final wish and was buried inside his beloved Morris Minor. A huge grave was dug and a large crowd gathered to watch the two lowered into the ground.

Sanford and his wife decided to pick out two burial plots. They went to the cemetery and discussed the locations with the manager of the facility. When Sanford inquired who his "neighbors" would be in a particular spot, his wife was horrified. She thought his concern was absurd. Later that week, she mentioned at dinner that she had played bridge that afternoon and they had all decided that they wanted to be buried next to each other. Hmmm . . . perhaps these thoughts are not quite so incongruous as they might at first appear.

OPEN/CLOSED CASKET

Since one of the stages in the grieving process is denial, viewing the body can be helpful and gives a sense of "closure." It is a poignant moment when the reality of death is recognized. Oftentimes close family members are present when a loved one dies, and it is very cathartic for them to spend as much time as they deem necessary with the body. Hospitals and those who transport bodies are much more aware of this need than they used to be. It is healthy to use this time wisely. Some people feel that a wider public display of the body in a funeral home is helpful. Still others see no need for any type of viewing, and they maintain viewing the body to be morbid. If the body is present in a closed casket, it is a wonderful opportunity to display a big beautiful photo or painting of the deceased. Whatever your choice, just be clear that avoiding the viewing is not intended to deny the loss. Again, it is a very personal choice, and there is no right or wrong.

EMBALMING

If an open casket is used at a funeral home, the body is usually embalmed. However, it is only in rare circumstances that this procedure is required by law. The United States is the only country where embalming has become customary. It was first used during the Civil War, when soldiers needed to be transported to their homes for burial. Embalming is not an environmentally friendly procedure, as toxic chemicals are used to replace bodily fluids for preservation. Refrigeration is a viable substitute for maintaining a body if a delay in the service is necessary. Make an educated choice.

CASKETS

Your choice of casket is limited only by your imagination. Traditionally, a casket is purchased from the funeral home, which has a variety of choices with different prices. If one of these caskets fills your needs, it is an expedient solution.

Caskets are also available online with an array of price tags. Trappist Caskets are beautifully constructed wooden caskets made by the monks at New Melleray Abbey from wood that comes from the monastery's own forest. The beautiful workmanship shows a preference for vintage, old-world joinery. Or there are discount casket warehouses that carry well-known brands at discount prices. Even Costco has more than a dozen caskets that can be shipped overnight.

CELEBRITY
EPITAPHS

I HAD A
LOVER'S
QUARREL
WITH THE
WORLD

–

ROBERT
FROST

If you prefer to use and enjoy your casket prior to your burial, there are more and more opportunities to do just that. A company called Casket Furniture will incorporate the casket's design into a casket sofa or coffin coffee table, or even a casket phone booth. A shop called Heaven on Earth is Britain's first designer death shop. These folks began making what they called "embodiment chests," which were actually dual-function caskets. Coffins were created with game boards inlaid in the top, linen chests for storage, bookcases, and CD holders. One custom coffin they supplied was called the Red Arrow jet coffin, designed to authentically replicate one of the Royal Air Force Acrobatic Team aircraft. However, the nose and wings had to be detachable to allow it to fit into the ground. Heaven on Earth has also created a coffin with a ship's wheel on the top. Environmentally-friendly caskets are also available. There are two styles of cardboard coffins: a Willow Coffin and a Bamboo Coffin. Customer comments range from "Coffins to die for …" to "Heaven on Earth really has put the fun back into funerals."

Frank Sinatra was buried with a bottle of Jack Daniels, a pack of Camel cigarettes, a Zippo lighter, and 10 dimes. He always carried ten dimes in case he needed to make an emergency phone call.

The North House Folk School in Grand Marais, Minnesota, offers a four-day course in building your own casket, if that interests you. And, of course, caskets can be decorated in any way you wish. A New England Patriots logo can adorn the side. Your school colors and insignia may be your theme. A watercolor of your garden may beautify the sides of your casket. Cowboys can have stirrups for handles. Again, your imagination sets the limits.

It is important to remember that, although there are coffins built to "last" with liners made of all sorts of materials, nothing is forever. Any container placed in the ground will eventually disintegrate. So don't be fooled by false claims.

Judy learned that she had a limited time to live. So she bought a plain pine coffin and put it in her room. She then gathered up markers, paints, and wood burners, and invited each of her friends to come work on decorating it. Each enjoyed a special time with her as they added their personal touch. It was a real tribute to her living memory.

CREMATION

Cremation is not a new practice, as there are references to it in both the Old and New Testaments. It is a process by which the body is placed in a retort—a specially designed furnace—and reduced to bone fragments through intense heat. These fragments are further reduced by a pulverizer, which formulates them into a consistent powder. The remaining ashes, or cremains, can weigh anywhere from three to nine pounds.

The popularity of cremation in the United States is increasing. In 1950 only 4 percent of the population in the United States chose to be cremated, while it had increased to almost 10 percent by 1980, and today stands at almost 30 percent. It is anticipated that by the year 2025, cremation will be used for disposition of the body in half of all U.S. deaths.

People choose cremation for diverse reasons. Some find the substantial monetary savings attractive. Others consider the environmental aspects, citing that ashes require less land use than do burials. Others are not comfortable with their body being placed in the Earth to decompose. And still others maintain that it both simplifies and dignifies this final event. The practical consideration of transporting a body home from a retirement location is also a factor. Again, it is a very personal decision.

The choice of a reputable crematory is critical. It may be one affiliated with your funeral home, or you may choose one on your own. If you do not use an experienced funeral home for direction, you can consult the Cremation Association of North America for guidance. There are many items to consider when making this choice. For one, you might inquire whether family members may be present during cremation. There are independent and discounted crematories sprouting up around the country. Many stringent policies and procedures are being imposed nationally, as there have been recent cases of laws being disregarded with rather horrific consequences. Ashes have been treated with disrespect and have been mixed up with others. Consider your preferences, get references, and investigate the crematory thoroughly.

If a traditional wake with a visitation and open casket is to take place before a cremation, a casket is needed. One may be rented for viewing, or an inexpensive liner may be purchased and then placed in a rented casket. If cremation takes place before the wake, an empty casket with a closed lid may be displayed. Or a wake may be eliminated all together.

As funerals become more flexible and religious restrictions diminish, it is probable that cremations will continue to increase.

URNS TO NECKLACES

Following the cremation, cremains are given to a person designated previously. Oftentimes, the cremains are placed in an urn or other container. Urns have historically been the vessel of choice.

There are Websites that offer quite diverse receptacles. Urns may be carved from Rocky Mountain Aspens from such locations as Silverthorne, Breckenridge, and Telluride. Custom containers in the shape of a cowboy boot, a golf bag, or a racecar are available. Containers may be engraved with the image of a fisherman or a hunter. Materials can vary from bronze to copper, from marble to wood, or even coconut shells. For those who wish to never be separated from their loved one, there are Companion Urns that will hold the cremains of two people. For those wishing to be outdoors, there are wind chimes as well as birdbaths that will hold a portion of your ashes. You might even have a favorite blue bottle on the kitchen windowsill that you would prefer to use to store your human ashes.

Another option is cremation jewelry. Necklaces may be fashioned to hold a portion of ashes around your neck. It is even possible to take the remaining carbon from cremains and create a low-grade industrial diamond for approximately $2,500. Again, the choices are limited only by your imagination.

ASHES TO ASHES

Scattering ashes is an old ritual that offers many alternatives. You may wish to have your ashes left in one spot or in a number of locations. Some folks may want to have a portion of their cremains scattered over the mountains where they skied, some alongside a spouse near their home, and then some over their birthplace. Permission must be granted to leave ashes on public property, or private property other than your own. Also, scattering ashes at sea is regulated by a Federal Code, which specifies that they must be thrown into ocean waters at least three miles from shore.

You may arrange to have your cremains placed in a container constructed out of environmentally safe materials and submerged, to be a part of an artificial underwater reef. These reefs are being constructed all over the world to replenish life in the ocean by encouraging the growth of coral and feeding fish.

For the more adventuresome, Space Services Inc. offers the option of being launched into space. A portion of the cremated remains is placed in a flight container. When the date is set for the space shot, families and friends are invited to a pre-launch memorial service and the actual liftoff. A keepsake DVD is also included, as is your biographical sketch on the company's Website.

Hunter Thompson, the American journalist, had his ashes blown from a cannon across his ranch in Colorado. And the *Chicago Tribune* ran an article about people who have subtly had their ashes sprinkled over the Ivy at Wrigley Field during a Cubs game or while on a tour of the park. Your ashes may be left where your heart once lived.

CELEBRITY
EPITAPHS

... IF I TAKE
THE WINGS
OF THE
MORNING
AND DWELL
IN THE
UTTERMOST
PARTS OF THE
SEA ...

–

ANNE AND
CHARLES
LINDBERGH

Or you can choose to go out with a bang! Your cremains can be loaded into specially modified fireworks and become part of a radiant display on a beach at sundown. A memorial service can be held first, followed by a beautifully choreographed fireworks display, accompanied by music of your choice.

ALKALINE HYDROLYSIS

As an alternative to burial or cremation, alkaline hydrolysis is one of the first truly innovative ideas to come along in the funeral industry for quite some time. Rather than burning the body, this process dissolves it in lye, leaving an environmentally safe liquid that can be safely flushed down the drain. Proponents of this method point out that there are much more troubling things, like blood and the spillover from embalming fluids, that routinely flow into sewage treatment plants.

Not only does alkaline hydrolysis eliminate the need for burial space, but it also does away with cremation emissions. A dry bone residue that is similar in volume and appearance to cremains is left and can be returned to the family if desired.

Originally the process was developed to dispose of animal carcasses, but it is meeting with substantial resistance for human use. It is legal in Minnesota and New Hampshire, but was voted down in New York, where it was nicknamed the "Hannibal Lector bill." It will be interesting to watch the evolution of alkaline hydrolysis.

CRYONICS

If you are not ready to cash in your chips when Mother Nature comes calling, you can always opt to give cryonics a try. This is the science that preserves the human body through ultra-cold temperatures in the hope that the future will have the technology to restore it to good health. Since 1967, more than one hundred people have been cryopreserved, and more than one thousand people have arranged to give cryonics a try.

Today modern medicine preserves human embryos for years, and can stop the heart and other organs for up to an hour, and then restart them. Cryonics cools cells and adds high concentrations of chemicals that allow very little ice formation, thereby preserving the basic structure of the cells without actually freezing them. The organization contends that preserving cell structures with such integrity will allow them to recover with the aid of future technology.

The definition of death is continually redefined. It used to be that death was said to take place when the heart stopped beating. Today death is believed to occur several minutes after the heart ceases to beat. Cryonics maintains that these "arbitrary" pronouncements of death will become obsolete, and that the vital signs, which define death today, will be changed as technology advances. Their final argument is that cryonics patients are not really dead, and that future discoveries will allow the cells to be revived.

The Alcor Life Extension Foundation, a nonprofit organization located in Scottsdale, Arizona, is the world leader in cryonics. The foundation was established in 1972 and is going strong. After all, who really does know what tomorrow may bring?

> **Odd Deaths**
>
> THOMAS JEFFERSON
> 1826
> He died on the 50th anniversary of the signing the Declaration of Independence, and on the same day as John Adams

DONATION

Donating your body or organs to science after death is becoming increasingly accepted. If you are not working with a funeral home, it is imperative to investigate any institution you are considering. There are numerous agencies that are in place to facilitate both whole body as well as tissue and organ donations.

The Anatomy Gifts Registry (AGR) is a nonprofit whole-body donation registry. This organization has hundreds of participating researchers worldwide whose involvement offsets their operating expenses. Not all willed-body donation programs have the stringent guidelines that control this organization. The cremated remains of the body are returned within two to four weeks at no cost to the family.

Medical schools are always in need of body donations. The study of anatomy comes first in many curriculums and serves as a foundation for other medical courses. It is increasingly necessary for physicians and other biomedical students to conduct special anatomical studies and research. The support from the general public is greatly appreciated. And again, cremains will be returned to the donor's family.

Individual organs may also be donated as transplants to living patients. The United States Congress established the Organ Procurement and Transplantation Network (OPTN), which links all the professionals involved in the donation and transplantation system. AGR also works with local organ banks to offer organs to the living.

LifeLegacy Foundation is a federally approved nonprofit foundation that accepts organ and tissue donations. These donations are targeted toward the advancement of scientific research and medical education. LifeLegacy will transport the donor from anywhere in the continental United States, file the death certificate, and return the cremated bodily remains within two to three weeks. The Foundation even offers a "family support" coordinator who assists families before and after the donation. All this is done at no cost to the family.

A critical element in the donation decision is communicating your wish to your family. They should understand your beliefs and motives, and hopefully, they will feel a sense of purpose from their loss. Contact the agency of your choice and document the required information.

We make a living by what we get. We make a life by what we give.
—Sir Winston Churchill (1874–1965)

IMPORTANCE OF ROOTS

Another consideration to keep in mind is that your survivors need a place to visit to be "with" you to celebrate and honor your memory. A burial plot may have a granite headstone in a local cemetery or be found with a GPS at a Green cemetery. If you choose cremation, it might seem pragmatic to scatter all your ashes and be "done with it." However, this can be difficult for your survivors. At least a portion of your ashes should be interred with a marker of some kind, even something as simple as an engraved stone under a special tree. This provides an actual physical location for your survivors to visit. To anticipate the needs of your loved ones when you are gone is vital.

An old monk was once asked why he cared for ancient graves, and why he cleaned the stones to preserve the writings carved there. His reply was simple: "They still have their names. They will always have their names."

    —Gregory and Suzanne Wolfe,
        publishers of the journal, *Image*

CELEBRITY
EPITAPHS

QUOTH
THE RAVEN,
"NEVERMORE."
-
EDGAR
ALLEN
POE

DOROTHY CECIL

Unmarried as yet

Dorothy Cecil
Wimbledon, England c. 1900

JOHN PENNY
Reader,
If cash thou art in want of any
Dig 6 feet deep;
And thou wilt find a Penny

–

Wimborne, England

IV.

CEMETERIES

Cemeteries are not all equal. They can be exquisite public parks with rolling hills, panoramic gardens, and beautifully sculpted marble and granite. They are gathering spots for locals to walk and enjoy natural landscapes. Prior to art museums, cemeteries were a kind of "museum without walls," as their carvings and headstones displayed beautiful work. There are any number of reasons why people visit cemeteries. In the historic Oakland Cemetery in Atlanta, folks visit the grave of "Bobby" Jones, the great golfer, and leave golf balls for good luck. And, if you pay for a tour of Oakland Cemetery, you will be eligible for $5 off your bill at Six Feet Under, the catfish restaurant across the street.

For centuries burials took place in graveyards behind local churches. As space became sparse, the idea of relegating a specific piece of land for burial was created. Within the United States, the first cemetery—the word is derived from the Greek, meaning "sleeping place"—was Mount Auburn in Boston. In the late nineteenth century it was one of the most popular tourist attractions in the city. Mount Auburn was the first self-perpetuating rural garden landscape of its type. Paying for a burial plot was a new idea, and as the cemetery flourished and worked economically, others sprang up around the country. When the New York legislature was exploring the idea of creating a park in the center of the city, it was Mount Auburn that was used as a model. The legislature proposed that Central Park be just like Mount Auburn, without the headstones!

Cemeteries are wonderful spots for thoughtful reflection, timely perspectives, and even marriage proposals. The sanctified ground creates a very special atmosphere.

TYPES OF CEMETERIES

Cemeteries come in many shapes, styles, and sizes. Profit, not-for-profit, and government-sponsored are the financial varieties. Churches and fraternal organizations are likely to own the not-for-profit cemeteries. Oftentimes churches also have memorial gardens on their grounds to hold cremains. Municipal cemeteries are run by local government agencies. Private cemeteries sell plots that are run by endowment care funds. If considering such a cemetery, investigate these funds and make certain that they are adequately endowed to self-perpetuate after all the plots have been sold. There are also national cemeteries. These plots are available to veterans, their spouses, and usually their minor children. These plots are free; they are given as an honor for military service.

> *Hugh Hefner bought the plot next to Marilyn Monroe's because he wanted to be buried next to "the most beautiful woman who ever lived." She was Playboy's first centerfold.*

Hollywood Forever in Hollywood, California, is quite an innovative cemetery. Founded in 1899 and formerly known as The Hollywood Memorial Park Cemetery, it holds the remains of Rudolph Valentino, Jayne Mansfield, Tyrone Power, Peter Lorre, and Cecil B. DeMille, among others. The cemetery was left unattended and was in a state of disrepair for years. In 1998 it was purchased and refurbished to its original splendor. Hollywood Forever has introduced some unique services. The chapel is web-wired so that any service may be viewed live worldwide. Hollywood Forever also has a production company that creates LifeStories, a video of your life. These LifeStories are stored in their Library of Lives and may be viewed at kiosks located throughout the cemetery. In the summer, outdoor films are shown on the side of Rudolph Valentino's mausoleum. Whether a cemetery with these amenities is on the cutting edge of the future or merely an oddity of the times remains to be seen.

Show me your cemeteries, and I will tell you what kind of people you have.
　　　—Benjamin Franklin (1706–1790),
　　　　　American statesman, scientist,
　　　　　philosopher, printer, writer, and inventor

ALL-INCLUSIVE CEMETERIES

Large corporations are buying up small local cemeteries, and some have started selling not only burial plots but funeral services as well. They sell caskets, and offer funeral services in on-site chapels as well as at the graveside. It is important to know that these cemeteries are not controlled by the same regulations as funeral homes. The full disclosures on price and services imposed on funeral homes are not in effect at these cemeteries. Perhaps the best way to investigate these corporations is to contact the Chamber of Commerce, Better Business Bureau, or find referrals from others.

GREEN CEMETERIES

A new, somewhat radical, and yet very ancient type of cemetery is the burgeoning "green cemetery." In green burials, an un-embalmed body is placed in the earth in a biodegradable box or shroud. Green Endings in the United Kingdom manufactures what might well be the most eco-friendly coffin on the market; it is constructed solely of recycled newspapers.

The concept is that the body decomposes, becomes rich fertilizer, and enriches the soil and ecosystem naturally. This environmentally friendly form of burial can actually be used to conserve land. People pay to be buried in a parcel of land, and the money garnered is put toward restoring the remaining land. If customers want any sort of plantings, they have to be native plants. The natural habitat of this open space is thus retained, and it can be used as a park or recreational area. No monuments or markers mar the view. A GPS system is implemented to assist visitors in finding their loved ones' burial location.

The Green Burial movement started in the United Kingdom and now has approximately 150 sites. There are about twenty Green Burial cemeteries being developed across the United States. Not surprisingly, northern California is the most active location. Forever Fernwood, a Green Cemetery being developed in Mill Valley, California, by Tyler Cassity, has received quite a lot of attention. Mr. Cassity maintains that Green Burial is a vehicle to save the planet. He defines each person as a "tiny little seed bank" in the ecosystem.

It's not enough to be a corpse anymore. Now you have to be a politically correct corpse.
　　—Thomas Lynch, Michigan funeral
　　　　　director and poet

HEADSTONES

Headstones mark holy ground where a body is laid and a life is honored. Early headstones were made of slate, and oftentimes left a moral message. Later marble was utilized, but it too disintegrated over time. Currently granite is used, and frequently the headstones portray some aspect of immortality, be it an obelisk or heavenly looking angels. At the beginning of the twentieth century, folks could purchase a headstone from the Sears-Roebuck Catalog.

Headstones, or markers, that are flush with the grass are found in memorial parks, which gives an open feeling to the space. Other cemeteries use both flush and upright stones. There often are restrictions on types of headstones allowed in various cemeteries, so consider that fact when choosing a cemetery.

Although there are traditional headstone styles, there is great potential for personalization. Examples of unique granite memorials abound at Hope Cemetery in Barre, Vermont, next to the Rock of Ages quarries. There is a giant living room chair, ostensibly representing the deceased's favorite piece of furniture. There are also a granite soccer ball, a racecar, an airplane, and even a full-sized bed with two people in it. So, create your own. Entire books have been written that provide step-by-step instructions for fashioning long-lasting, beautiful stone monuments. Now that's personal!

If you don't find it in the index, look very carefully through the entire catalogue.
>
> —Sears-Roebuck Consumer's Guide, 1897

EPITAPHS

If ever there were a personalization opportunity, it is your epitaph, your final say. Final. Epitaphs give you a measure of immortality, a bridge between you and those to come. The message may be profound, or humorous, or tell a story.

An English teacher might choose Hamlet's last line, "The rest is silence." Quite an appropriate sentiment for a headstone, and befitting his position. A barfly might lament, "There must be some mistake. I still have a tab running."

> **Odd Deaths**
>
> TINY TIM
> 1996
> He died after
> falling off a stage
> at a ukulele
> festival

Writing epitaphs was once great fodder for witty parlor games, but today it has come to be considered slightly morbid. Turn back the hands of time and create some prose for your headstone as a last hurrah.

In lapidary inscriptions a man is not upon oath.
>
> —Samuel Johnson (1709–1784),
> English author, critic, and lexicographer

HONEST LAWYER

Sir John Strange

Here lies an honest lawyer
And that is strange

DENTIST

Stranger tread
This ground with gravity.
Dentist Brown
Is filling his last cavity

HOUSEWIFE

Dear friends I am going
Where washing ain't done
Or cooking or sewing:
Don't mourn for me now
Or weep for me never:
For I do nothing
Forever and ever!

AUCTIONEER

Going!
Going!
Gone!

ATTORNEY

The defense rests

HANGED MAN

Who died for the want
Of another breath

AUDLTEROUS HUSBAND

Gone, but not forgiven

COAL MINER

Gone Underground for Good

SPINSTER POSTMISTRESS

Returned—Unopened

I AM READY TO MEET MY MAKER

Whether my Maker is prepared

for the great ordeal of meeting me

is another matter.

Winston Churchill

Here lies Pa
Pa liked women
Ma caught Pa
in with two
swimmin'
Here lies Pa

V.

TYPE OF SERVICE

The closest bonds we will ever know are bonds of grief. The deepest community one of sorrows.

—Cormac McCarthy (1933–), American
novelist, *All the Pretty Horses*

Funerals can be as varied as there are personalities on the planet. Sing your own special song—make it yours. This service should be a reflection of you, your lifestyle, and your personal dignity. An honest and thorough evaluation of your life will be your guiding light in making these decisions.

Funeral services can be held in a church, in a funeral home chapel, by a lake, or in a pub. The body may be present or not; the casket may be open or closed. If cremation is the choice, cremains may or may not be present. The service can be led by the Pope, your lifelong minister, a funeral director, a hired celebrant, or a friend. It may take place immediately at your death, or a memorial service may be held later at any convenient time. Traditionally, memorial services are held without the body present. Those are lots of choices. Open your mind, shed conventional wisdom if you like, and create a service that speaks for you.

CHURCH

For many, having a funeral in a church is like having turkey at Thanksgiving. It is just quite simply what you do. The clergy from your church or synagogue will traditionally lead the service in your house of worship and, being familiar with you, will be able to put together a meaningful and personal service. However, you certainly still have many choices within this framework.

There are other reasons to have a funeral service in a house of worship. Many people have belonged to a congregation, but they have moved or otherwise lost touch. However, a return to a former place of worship may offer reassurance and familiarity. Or, if a close relative is comfortable at a particular parish house, and you are not averse to the idea, it can be a great comfort to them to be in a recognizable and meaningful place.

> After a lovely service in his lifelong, beloved church, with the choir singing all his favorite hymns, and his friends reading all his favorite Bible passages, Randall's family and friends walked out into the beautiful churchyard. His old kite-flying buddy Bill was out there, holding a big beautiful kite soaring up in the air. He invited each of the attendees to stop, take hold of the line, and offer up a silent prayer for Randall. It was a powerful moment for all.

FUNERAL HOME

Another alternative for your service is to use the funeral home as your focal point. Often funeral homes have small chapels or attractive gathering halls for services. Funeral directors are beginning to offer more and more meaningful and personalized funerals. Courses such as Bill Bates's Life Appreciation Training Seminars train funeral directors to go beyond their traditional roles. Besides being funeral arrangers, they can be personalization specialists. Some funeral directors will even write your entire service or step into the master of ceremonies role in conjunction with a clergy person or other professional.

Some funeral homes are going all out to create more far-reaching services. There is a mortuary in Las Vegas that offers funeral backdrops such as giant playing cards, oversized dice, and a huge slot machine. Even gargantuan casino chips and a "Fabulous Las Vegas" sign are available. Choices abound!

HUMANIST SERVICES

A humanist funeral service is one centered around a non-supernatural force. Their philosophy rejects the idea of personal immortality and sees death as a real end. Humanists are not averse to emotion at a ceremony, but they do discourage sentimentality and boastful behavior. The three main points of their philosophy revolve around nature, death as a natural process, and the ideals of human living. They maintain that human life on Earth, rather than an afterlife, is the supreme goal. While the humanist service is devoid of spiritual and eternal life references, it may still be quite personal and compelling.

CELEBRANTS

Another alternative for your funeral service is to invite a celebrant to officiate. According to the In-Sight Institute, the definition of a celebrant is: A person—male or female, clergy or layperson—who seeks to meet the needs of families during their time of loss. They serve by providing a funeral service that is personalized to reflect the personality and lifestyle of the deceased.

Celebrants are widespread throughout Australia and New Zealand. Their popularity is growing across the United States, where training is done through Doug Manning's In-Sight Institute. A celebrant plans, writes, and carries out the entire service for the family. Guided by their own code of ethics, celebrants provide top-level and professional funeral services.

At the time of a loved one's death, a celebrant arrives and meets privately with the family for a "Story Telling Time." By meeting with the family and actively participating in their grieving process, celebrants create a safe place for the family's initial grieving process to begin. As the celebrant hears the stories and memories of the deceased, survivors are experiencing a therapeutic process just by talking. Being encouraged to remember together creates an intimate

CELEBRITY
EPITAPHS

I WILL NOT
BE BACK
RIGHT
AFTER THIS
MESSAGE
-
MERV
GRIFFIN

atmosphere where people bond together and begin the new transitions that the death has created.

This family meeting also gives the celebrant a real feeling for the life of the deceased. The celebrant is trained to guide and solicit personal suggestions from families, to help them vocalize the actual significance of the person who has died, and to recognize the importance of participation by loved ones before and during the service. These and other steps begin the healing process right away. The celebrant will then plan, write, and create a service including, when desired, readings and words from family members and friends. By incorporating special music, writing the eulogy, and planning ceremonial acts to be used during the service, the celebrant creates a personalized service. If a religious service is planned for the day of the funeral, a celebrant may also conduct a personalized service at the wake the night before. Their flexibility and desire to help out in any way make them an invaluable asset.

Celebrants oftentimes work with a funeral home, but many are free agents. They can be found through the In-Sight Institute Certified Celebrants at www.insightbooks.com. You would be well advised to find a celebrant who has been certified.

An elderly woman, mother of five, lived a long and wonderful life, and died quietly at home at age 89. When the children gathered, they remarked that she really had very few friends remaining, and there really was not much to say at her funeral. Luckily, one of her offspring had thought to call a celebrant to meet with the group. The more the group talked, the more loving memories they shared. The one universal memory that all had in common were her unbelievably delicious cookies. The celebrant put together a short service that used her recipes as analogies to the other aspects of her life. The children ultimately put together a cookbook of "Mom's Famous Cookies." The inscription inside read, "Mom even smelled like cookies."

HOME DEATH

Anyone who stays away from a death because of distress, because the physical aspects can be so very unpleasant, will turn out to have missed the one experience of a lifetime which can make known the true heights of love.

—Evelyn Francis Capel (1911–), author,
priest, and counselor

One unique variation from the traditional funeral is the rather extreme, yet truly old-fashioned, home death alternative. Rather than having the body immediately handed over to the professional staff of a funeral director at death, the body is cared for by the loved ones at home. It is referred to as "after-death care." The body is either laid in bed or put on display in the parlor, as was the custom years ago. This concept is not dissimilar to the growing practice of choosing to give birth at home rather than at a hospital. Care is provided personally, rather than by a salaried third party.

Caring for a loved one's body for anywhere from one to five days after death gives the family time to assimilate the loss into their lives and assures them that the body is being treated respectfully and lovingly. The body is usually packed in dry ice, and an around-the-clock vigil is kept at the side of the deceased. Actually, the term "wake" comes from a time when people literally dropped dead in the fields and were carried into the parlor and laid out. However, no one was ever entirely certain the person was indeed dead until days had passed, and the person had not reawakened!

With a body at home, people can visit the house, view the body, and have personal time. Obviously, another great benefit is lower cost. At some point a ceremony can be held with people gathered around the body. Candle lightings, readings, and music can all be meaningful parts of this time. The body is then removed and either buried, cremated, or donated. For some this direct involvement with every aspect of caring for their loved ones is a gift and an occasion for healing.

Even with home death, there are reasons to hire a funeral home to handle details such as death certificates and other legal details. However, the law does not require professionals to do these tasks. If you wish, you may leave the instructions about handling this process for your survivors. Lisa Carlson has written a book, *Caring for Your Own Dead*, with many poignant examples of this ritual as well as detailed information on state-by-state regulations. Two organizations, Crossings and Final Passages, are quite involved with the home death experience, and they have extensive and detailed information on dealing with after-death care at home.

> When Steve died, his neighbors and friends went over to his home to pay their respects to his widow and children. Many were a bit taken aback to learn that they could also pay their respects to Steve at the same time. His body lay on his bed in the master bedroom, dressed in his favorite fishing clothes, surrounded by flowers and burning candles, with his favorite classical music selections playing. His wife Arlene had made the decision to care for him after his death. After three days of grieving at home, she felt she was ready to let go of his body. She understood and accepted the finality and reality of his death. She found caring for Steve a rewarding final act of love.

VIKING FUNERALS

If you have a sense of the dramatic, and cling hard and fast to ancient traditions, a Viking funeral might be a perfect choice. The Vikings believed that this funeral form guaranteed immortality. A corpse is loaded into a ship or smaller craft as monetary restrictions dictate. The boat is pushed off from shore at sunset and lit on fire with a flaming arrow. If the color of the fire and the sunset match, it proves that the deceased led a good life.

This type of funeral appeared quite appealing in the 1988 film *Rocket Gibraltar* with Burt Lancaster, but it may leave something to be desired in real life. Good to keep an open mind, however.

The art of living well and the art of dying well are one.
— Epicurus (341 B.C.–270 B.C.),
Greek philosopher

CELEBRITY
EPITAPHS

THERE
GOES THE
NEIGHBOR-
HOOD

-

RODNEY
DANGERFIELD

Odd Deaths

BRANDON LEE
Actor
1993
He was accidentally shot during the filming of *The Crow*.
The gun used in the filming mistakenly had a dummy round lodged in the barrel, and when it was used in the scene, a blank cartridge was driven into Lee's abdomen.

I TOLD YOU

I WAS SICK

Round Rock, Texas

Here lies THE KID
We planted him raw,
He was quick on the trigger
But slow on the draw

–

Silver City, Neada

VI.

FUNDAMENTALS

Planning your actual funeral service may seem a bit daunting. But, as with most things, if you just begin at the beginning and develop ideas around a core, it will build on itself and become clear to you as you go along.

PERSONAL PARTICULARS

Details create the big picture.
　　—Sanford I. Weill (1933–), banker and financier

Since one of your key intentions is to aid your loved ones with details concerning your funeral, it is imperative to leave them with the vital details of your life. The real nuts and bolts of your days need to be in written form and accessible to those who will need it.

There are many formal documents available that articulate exactly what information is necessary for your loved ones. These forms are available at funeral homes, from local religious organizations, and online. There are also entire books that offer guidance in organizing and recording these details. The minimal time it will take you to fill out such forms will save exponential time for your survivors.

Another thoughtful detail is a list of who should be contacted at your death. It is not an easy time for your family, and any information that gives them relief and avoids unconscious slights is invaluable.

Here are examples of required information:

PERSONAL HISTORY

Full Name: Maiden Name:

Address:

City: State: Zip:

Telephone:

Birthplace:

Date of Birth:

Social Security Number:

Marital Status: Married   Single

                                 Divorced   Widowed

                                 Never Married

Spouse:

Father's Name:

Mother's Name:

Mother's Maiden Name:

Children:

Stepchildren:

Education:

Occupation:

Religious Affiliation:

Military Information:

Clubs and Organizations:

PERSONAL RECORDS

Bank Accounts:

Safe Deposit Box:

Location of Key:

Insurance Policies:

Real Estate:

Stocks and Bonds:

Assets and Liabilities:

Leave this information with a trusted member of your family ... or two!

Let each of us become all that he was created capable of being.
—Thomas Carlyle (1795–1881), Scottish author,
essayist, and historian

PERSONAL ASSESSMENT

Before composing the final mural of our lives, perhaps we should begin by sketching a light outline. Clients of funeral directors who have taken Bill Bates' Life Appreciaiton course are asked to fill out a form that includes details about their lives that are both factual as well as spiritual. Some of the questions include the following:

What accomplishments do you feel good about?
What are some of your fondest memories?
What people have had the greatest impact on your life?
What things would you like to do before you die?
What people would you like to say goodbye to?

If you could live your life over again:
      what would you spend less time doing?
      what would you spend more time doing?

What would you do if you could do anything before
      you die?
What are the things you always wanted to do but have not?
What behaviors and attitudes have held you back?
What behaviors and attitudes do you admire in others?
What things have given you the most pleasure in life?
What causes and beliefs are you most passionate about?
What is the most fun you have ever had?
What are you most proud of?

The thoughtful answers to these questions will give you a vivid outline from which to arrange your funeral details. And, perhaps equally important, completing it will give you a new perspective on your life today. These and all other introspections that crop up during your funeral planning process may well help you to live more fully and realize all of your goals more completely.

CELEBRITY
EPITAPHS

GO AWAY—
I'M ASLEEP
-
JOAN
HACKET

The greater danger for most of us lies not in setting our aim too high and falling short, but in setting our aim too low, and achieving our mark.

—Michelangelo (1475–1564), sculptor,
painter, architect, and poet

OUTLINE

Generally, a service has the following components:

Prelude
Introduction
Music
Life story
Music
Scripture, prayer, or readings
Words from family or friends
Music
Eulogy
Closing ceremony
Postlude

Within this general outline, you can now begin to plan your service so that it expresses your spirit. Leaving information in written form will help your loved ones put together a beautiful service all about you.

One suggestion, based on personal experience, is not to encourage an "open mike" at your service. Although it might seem like a creative way for people to express themselves in a freeform manner, it most often does not work well. Remarks that have been thoughtfully written out and edited have a much better chance of creating a meaningful and evocative affair than random remarks. At the gathering after the service, people will have an opportunity to speak and express themselves.

Intriguing Funeral Processions

Alpha 4 X 4 Funeral Services in Great Britain offers a Land Rover Hearse for the final journey to the cemetery. They propose that this service allows the deceased to make a personal statement about his style and individuality.

A Hawg Heaven Hearse is available for motorcycle enthusiasts. It is a nineteenth-century style hearse pulled by a three-wheeled motorcycle. The procession will follow the decedent's favorite roads en route to the cemetery.

On display at the National Museum of Funeral History is a 1916 Packard Funeral bus. It was built to carry not only a casket, but the pallbearers and up to 20 mourners. It met its demise while climbing a hill in San Francisco. The weight of all the people in the back caused it to tip over and sent the people and the casket into the street. It was immediately retired.

Sum quod eras

"I am as you will be"

Here lies the body of
JONATHON BLAKE
Stepped on the Gas
Instead of the Brake

–

Uniontown, Pennsylvania

VII.

SERVICE BASICS

READINGS

Language exerts hidden power, like a moon on the tides.
—Rita Mae Brown (1944–), U.S. author and
social activist

Your funeral is one of the last times you have to communicate your personal beliefs and philosophies. The readings you choose should reflect your voice. Readings have traditionally come from the Bible or other religious texts. However, anywhere you find meaningful words is fine. Poetry and verse speak volumes. Song lyrics can hold wonderful messages. There are no rules.

If you are a spiritual person, the New and Old Testaments are a treasure. Perhaps the Twenty-Third Psalm is seemingly always read. And perhaps with good reason. Don't throw the baby out with the bath water.

TWENTY-THIRD PSALM

"The Lord is my Shepherd: I shall not want.
He maketh me to lie down in green pastures;
He leadeth me beside the still waters, he restoreth my soul.
He leadeth me in the paths of righteousness for His name's sake,
Yea, though I walk through the valley of the shadow of death
I will fear no evil; For thou art with me;
Thy rod and Thy staff they comfort me ..."

A message of support for your loved ones is a gift as well:

MISS ME, BUT LET ME GO

When I come to the end of the road
And the sun has set for me,
I want no rites in a gloom filled room,
Why cry for a soul set free?

Miss me a little ... but not too long,
And not with your head bowed low,
Remember the love that once we shared,
Miss me, but let me go.

For this is a journey that we all must take,
And each must go alone,
It's all part of the master plan,
A step on the road to home.

When you are lonely and sick of heart,
Go to the friends we know
And bury your sorrows in doing good deeds,
Miss me, but let me go.
　　　　　—Anonymous

The following was printed on the funeral program of the much beloved mother of Queen Elizabeth ll:

You can shed tears that she is gone
or you can smile because she has lived.

You can close your eyes and pray that she'll come back
or you can open your eyes and see all she's left.

Your heart can be empty because you can't see her
or you can be full of the love you shared.

You can turn your back on tomorrow and live yesterday
or you can be happy for tomorrow, because of yesterday.

You can remember her, and only that she's gone
or you can cherish her memory, and let it live on.

You can cry and close your mind, be empty and turn your back
or you can do what she'd want: smile, open your eyes, love and go on.

—Anonymous

MUSIC

A song will outlive all sermons in memory.
—Henry Giles (1814–1880), English author

Music is the soul of language.
—Max Heindel (1865–1919), Christian
occultist, astrologer, and mystic

There is a theory that music existed even before words as a form of communication. You would be hard-pressed to create as powerful an emotion with words as with music. The music you choose has the potential to dominate the entire spirit of your funeral. Music can be played before the service begins, and interspersed throughout. A soloist may be asked to perform. Or you may choose to have songs sung in unison to encourage participation. A sound system can easily accommodate any music you would like to play during the service.

There are traditional hymns that have been played for years and years at funerals. And again, with good reason. They are powerful and filled with significance. Is "Amazing Grace"

overplayed? Perhaps. However, it could also be argued that
1 Corinthians 13 is an overused verse at weddings. Yet these
words are timeless:

> Amazing grace, how sweet thou art
> That saved a wretch like me
> I once was lost but now I'm found
> Twas blind but now I see
> Twas grace that brought me safe thus far
> And grace will lead me home.

You know what music you like, and which lyrics inspire
you. If the Golden Oldies of the '50s never quite got out
of your system, then pick your favorites and play them.
Remember Neil Sedaka's "Stairway to Heaven"?

> I'll build a stairway to heaven
> I'll climb to the highest star
> I'll build a stairway to heaven
> 'Cause heaven is where you are!
>   —"Stairway to Heaven"

Broadway show tunes often have evocative words. The
Sound of Music included "Climb Ev'ry Mountain."

> Climb ev'ry mountain,
> Ford every stream,
> Follow every rainbow
> Till you find your dream.
>   —"Climb Ev'ry Mountain"

Does the University of Michigan fight song define you?
Let's hear "The Victors"!

> Hail to the victors valiant, hail to the conquering
> heroes
> Hail! Hail! to Michigan, The champions of the west.

If country and western flows through your veins, Joe Diffie's "Prop Me Up Beside the Jukebox" might be just the tune to make everyone remember you.

> Prop me up beside the jukebox when I die
> Lord I wanna go to heaven, but I don't wanna go tonight
> Fill my boots up with sand, put a stiff drink in my hand
> Prop me up beside the jukebox when I die.
> —"Prop Me Up Beside The Jukebox (If I Die)"

Lee Ann Womack's "I Hope You Dance" has lyrics that leave a poignant message for people.

> I hope you still feel small when you stand beside the ocean
> Whenever one door closes I hope one more opens
> Promise me that you'll give faith a fighting chance
> And when you get the choice to sit it out or dance
> I hope you dance
> —"I Hope You Dance"

Or the very simple "Rainbow Connection" might say it all for you.

> Someday we'll find it, the Rainbow Connection
> The lovers, the dreamers, and me.
> —"The Rainbow Connection"

Music is well said to be the speech of angels.
> —Thomas Carlyle (1795–1881) Scottish essayist, satirist, and historian

*After silence, that which comes nearest to expressing the inexpressible
is music.*
> —Aldous Huxley (1894–1963), British writer,
> Music at Night, 1931

FUNERAL PROCESSION

Even the procession to the cemetery can be memorable
and resound with your spirit. There are so many alternatives
to personalize this final procession. One woman drove the
hearse in her husband's funeral procession because he had
always insisted that she drive whenever they went out. An
elderly man had walked his golden retriever Sam throughout
his neighborhood for hours every day. Sam led his procession.
There was a fellow who had driven the local ice cream
truck in a small town for years. His procession was led by
his ice cream truck, and free Popsicles were distributed at his
graveside. These departed spirits were in attendance at their
respective funerals.

> The service for the first man in a small New
> England town to lose his life in the Iraq War drew
> quite a crowd both inside and outside the local
> Congregational Church. After the service, his casket
> was placed on a horse-drawn caisson. His immediate
> family walked directly behind the horse, followed by
> hundreds of local residents in a mile long procession
> to the local cemetery. There were folks along the
> entire route waving small American flags. An
> enormous flag was draped over the entrance to the
> cemetery as well. This procession will not soon be
> forgotten by anyone in town.

> Bob was the president of a motorcycle club. He
> had always instructed his friends to "make some
> noise" when they pulled out of his driveway. He

had made arrangements for a motorcycle hearse to carry his body to the cemetery. The sidecar made a detour past his house on the way to the cemetery with twenty-five motorcycles following it. As each motorcycle passed Bob's driveway, the rider gunned the engine, "making some noise," as a final tribute to him.

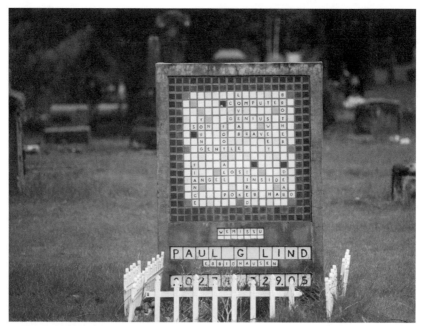

Lone Fir Cemetery   *Portland, Oregon*   *Steve Oswald*

Lancaster Cemetery
Lancaster, Indiana
Lisa Nightenhelse

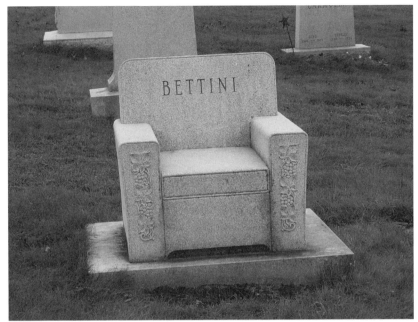

Hope Cemetery   *Barre, VT*   *William Alexander*

Hope Cemetery   *Barre, VT*   *William Alexander*

Hope Cemetery   *Barre, VT*   *William Alexander*

Hope Cemetery   *Barre, VT*   *William Alexander*

Hope Cemetery   *Barre, VT*   *William Alexander*

Hope Cemetery   *Barre, VT*   *William Alexander*

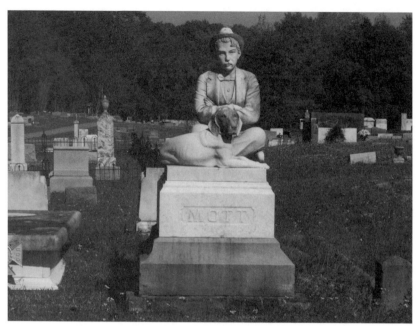

Crystal Springs Cemetery Crystal Springs, Mississippi   *Sally Garland*

Rosedale and Rosehill Cemetery   Linden, NJ   Ruth Clusman

Rose Hill Cemetery   Macon, GA   Nancy Dixon

Wyuka Cemetery   Bellevue, NE   Marta Dawes

Laurel Grove Memorial Park
Totowa, NJ
Anthony Sgobba

Highland Cemetery
Okemah, Oklahoma
Lisa Stiles

Expired Parking Meter

Outstanding Send-offs

Bill Hawkes was a great character from Marblehead, Massachusetts. He lived right next to Redd's Pond, a scenic little quarry behind Old Burial Hill. Among other things, he built cannons. He requested that his ashes be blasted across this little pond. Ten of his friends, each of whom owned one of his cannons, gathered on a beautiful afternoon and lined up with five on each side. Each loaded a portion of Bill's ashes into his canon, and at the exact same moment fired them into the pond.

HERE LIES EZEKIAL AIKLE

AGE 102

THE GOOD

DIE YOUNG

Ezekial Aikle
East Dalhousie Cemetery, Nova Scotia

Here lies ANN MANN
Who lived an old maid
But died an old MANN

–

London, England

VIII.

SERVICE ENHANCEMENTS

Beyond the basics of a funeral, there are a few enhancements that can greatly augment the personal touch of your service. These additions have the potential to make your thoughts and ideas stay with people long after they leave the funeral.

LIFE STORY LINE

Memory is the diary that we all carry around with us.
—Oscar Wilde (1854–1900), Irish dramatist,
novelist, and poet

A great place to start your planning process is to put together a factual time line of your life and then fill it in with interesting pieces of information. Let's say you were born in 1935. It might be fun to include some "current events" of that particular year. Who was president? When did you get a TV? What were the lives of your parents like? Did your grandfather remember the Civil War?

Pertinent facts about your childhood and schooling are also interesting. Probably not many of the folks in attendance were with you in second grade. Did you really have to be home before the streetlights went on? You climbed how far up that rock? The story of how you and your husband or wife met is certainly interesting to lots of people. It is so many of those details from years ago that shaped your life.

These memories can be woven into a meaningful piece to be read by a predetermined person at your funeral. All these pieces of information are a part of what makes you who you are.

PERSONAL MEMORIES

To live in hearts we leave behind is not to die.
— Thomas Campbell (1777–1844), Scottish poet

Next, share some memories. Certain memories are once-in-a-lifetime events: weddings, parties, vacations, and births. But many others are those small life experiences that happened every day at some point in your life. Maybe it was a silly TV show that you watched every night with your children. Maybe it was pulling lobster traps. Maybe it was Sunday mornings going to church. Maybe it was a pickup game of soccer on Saturday afternoons. Memories are made up of moments, not days. Recollections can be seemingly inconsequential, but on closer inspection they are full of meaning. And all those attending your service who were a part of these memories will be remarkably touched.

The other facts that shape you are your hobbies and recreational activities. Maybe you are one of those people who can't get to the golf course fast enough whenever the occasion arises. Maybe you are on your boat in any kind of weather. Do you work on bonsai trees in your spare time or build birdhouses? Have you knit scarves, hats, and mittens for everyone in your family? Do you make your own wine? Do you create beautiful jewelry? Do you tinker with cars? Do you play an instrument? Have you traveled to Europe, South America, and the South Pacific? Or do you just have a favorite town in northern Michigan that calls you back summer after summer? Have you always had dogs and cats? What were their names? How about that favorite sports team—do you have Chicago Cubs paraphernalia all over the house? Jot down these thoughts to be read and to give substance to your service.

Ann and Henry had traveled to the four corners of the earth during their lifetimes. When Henry passed away, Ann chose a dozen matchbooks from the assortment they had collected from their travels.

She then placed twelve candles in the front of the church and gave matches to their twelve nieces and nephews. When she called their names, each stepped forward, read the name and location on his or her matchbook, and lit a candle. It was a nice way to have the family participate, and collectively, it was a wonderful tribute to their personal memories.

HUMOR

Comedy is simply a funny way of being serious.
—Peter Ustinov (1921–2004), English actor
and author

There are very few things in life that are not improved with a bit of humor. Your family and friends have known and loved you for a lifetime and are probably quite familiar with your brand of humor. What could be nicer than to weave a bit of this humor into your service? People want to feel your presence, and humor is so personal that you will indeed be felt.

You can label your will as "A dead giveaway" if you are so inclined. Are you a real pun man? Let people know that you were "dying" to be at this service! Always the first with a new blonde joke? Leave them with the one about the blonde who was fired from the M&M factory for throwing away all the W's. Perhaps you share Woody Allen's sentiment, "I don't want to achieve immortality through my work ... I want to achieve it through not dying." Let your humor live on. Laughter and tears mix well.

He deserves paradise who makes his companions laugh.
—The Koran, the central religious text of Islam

PARTICIPATION

The only cure for grief is action.
—George Henry Lewes (1833–1911),
distinguished English society lawyer

Participation by your family and friends is a key component to a successful funeral, and it sets the healing process in motion. Involvement gives everyone a structure to show their love. Participation also helps to define the reality of the death. Though it may seem harsh, reality turns the grieving loose and releases feelings.

People can be involved in many different ways. Ask a friend to do a eulogy. It is an honor to be asked and may settle much angst. You might also ask a family member or friend to read a poem or verse that you hold dear to your heart. Having been asked to read a particular piece holds a real connection for that person. Someone might even be asked to sing or play a solo. The more personalized the service, the more it will mean and more beneficial it will be.

At this point it is important to note that too detailed a funeral plan can have an adverse effect. Some details should be left to the survivors to assure their participation. Leave some wiggle room for your survivors to fine-tune your plans a bit. Thoughtful planning will allow a number of people to participate to some extent.

When Beth's friend Karen died, there was a real void left. They had walked together every day for years and had faced so many of life's ups and downs together. One of their shared joys was gardening. Each had a spectacular garden. Beth, always one to keep busy, decided to put together small bags of seeds to give everyone at the funeral service to take home and plant. Not only was it a lovely remembrance

of Karen, but it served Beth well to feel she was
contributing to the service.

Do not protect yourself by a fence, but rather by your friends.
 —Czech proverb

PARTICIPATION BY CHILDREN

When making funeral plans, it is also important to consider
the children in your life, whether they be your grandchildren,
your nieces and nephews, or your favorite little neighbor
who feeds the cat. If handled with appropriate developmental
understanding, funerals experienced in childhood help
children to be less afraid of death as an adult.

Children should be included in a funeral service if it gives
them comfort. A youngster may want to play or sing their
mother's favorite song. Another may wish to recite a favorite
verse. These presentations may be taped or live. It is imperative
that children understand that their participation will not be
judged as a measure of their love for the deceased. They need
not participate in order to prove their affection. And be sure
to accept a child's decision regarding participation warmly
and lovingly.

Specific programs have been developed for children to
participate in at funeral homes. While adults are involved with
making arrangements, children have their own time to learn
about what they may see and hear and experience in the next
few days. Crafts and messages can be prepared to leave in the
casket. The Star Class is a particularly helpful plan. Children
meet with an adult for about 30 minutes and prepare for what
they might experience during a visitation, funeral, and the
burial process. They are also encouraged to create a personal
message or story through creative art projects.

Children may also help choose favorite photos for a
memory board. Be careful to choose photos that portray
happy times, and are ones that the child particularly likes.

Older children may wish to deliver a eulogy.

> Fran's children, Martha, Caleb, and Johnny, all
> spoke briefly at their father's funeral. The common
> message they shared was the lesson Fran had reiterated
> throughout his life, which was simply: "Try hard, and
> be nice." Although each one had diverse interests
> and a distinct personality, they all described how his
> lesson had influenced their personal life. Collectively
> it was a brilliant tribute to Fran.

A thoughtfully planned funeral service can be a great
inspiration to children. Demonstrating a life well lived is an
invaluable lesson for young minds. Be aware of the young
people, and include them appropriately.

Children require guidance and sympathy far more than instruction.
—Annie Sullivan (1866–1936), lifelong teacher
and companion to Helen Keller

CEREMONY

Another important component of a meaningful funeral
service is ceremony. Ceremonies are powerful, and they are a
wonderful way to involve people. A single candle lit by a loved
one is powerful, as are numerous candles burning together
to form community. Releasing butterflies or even doves has
become popular, along with balloon releases. Looking up to
the sky also lightens spirits.

Another thought is to hand each attendee an item that holds
significance for you as they arrive at your service. At some
point during the service, have everyone come forward and
either place the article in the casket or in a bowl or basket in
the front. Collectively, these items symbolize not only you, but
the connection of the community of people at your service.
Ceremonies honoring a person's individuality are poignant.

Susan was an avid gardener. She was truly at her best
with dirty fingernails. Whenever she went anywhere,
she inevitably had a beautiful bunch of flowers to
give away. As people entered for Susan's service, each
was handed a beautiful flower. At the close of the
ceremony, people were asked to place their flowers
on Susan's coffin to form a final beautiful bouquet.

CELEBRITY
EPITAPHS

TRADITIONS

JACK
LEMON IN

···

-

JACK
LEMON

Traditions hold power. As with music, traditions can speak
more effectively than even the most poignant words. If you
have certain traditions that are distinctly yours, incorporate
them into your service. Sharing these rituals can be incredibly
evocative. Consider carefully what would best convey your
spirit to your family and friends. And perhaps these rituals
will live on after you are gone.

Marilyn was widowed after sixty years of marriage.
She confided to her minister that she and her husband
had always held hands and said the Lord's Prayer
together at the end of each day. At the conclusion
of the service, Marilyn was escorted to the casket,
where she placed her hand over her husband's, and
the entire congregation stood and recited the Lord's
Prayer with her.

Henry David Thoreau
Concord, Massachusetts 1862

Remember Man, as you walk by
As you are now, so once was I
Remember this and follow me!

Found written on the tombstone:
To follow you I'll not consent
Until I know which way you went

–

England

IX.

SERVICE ACCESSORIES

The "piece de resistance" for your funeral is to put your personal stamp on all the visuals. Perhaps you haunted a local coffee shop every morning. By setting out a copy of "your" daily newspaper, along with "your" coffee mug, with a photo that had been taken one morning with you and all your morning friends, people will almost see you as they listen to your last thoughts.

LOCATION, LOCATION, LOCATION

So, if you are not required to have your funeral in an unfamiliar, cavernous church, or a dingy parlor with brocade chairs in a dark funeral home, the choices already seem better, don't they? Since your funeral is your own personal event, its location takes on a whole new meaning. If you are a hiker who loves the outdoors, maybe there is a spot along the Appalachian Trail that would be a lovely place for your family and friends to gather. Or perhaps your home is your castle, and you have worked and reworked every square inch of it. Wouldn't it be lovely to have everyone gathered right there? An avid gardener might be best felt in the midst of flowering grounds. And if you will be most vividly felt in your lifelong church, most assuredly hold it there. Gather where you belong.

Brian had been a zookeeper for his entire life. His real passion in life had been working with the animals. When Brian passed away, friends and family were invited to gather in a tent outside the zoo gates for a cocktail reception. They then boarded a waiting train and began a slow ride around the zoo, stopping at the bear pavilion, the lion pavilion, and finally at

the arboretum. At each stop, photographs that Brian
had taken of the various animals were on display,
and his wife and best friends gave meditations about
Brian and his life. Nowhere was Brian's presence felt
more than at his zoo.

FLOWERS

Earth laughs in flowers.
> —Ralph Waldo Emerson (1803–1882),
> U.S. essayist and poet

Flowers are another very personal choice and can even
be quite symbolic. Cosmos represent peace, irises signify
inspiration, and Forget-Me-Nots are sure to suggest
"remember me forever!"

Of course your individual preferences are most important.
If your friends walk in and see the tricolor carnations you
always found abhorrent, they will not only think you are not
there, they will hope you are not there. Don't let it happen.
If you want tulips, sunflowers, roses, or daisies, include that in
your preparations, and your wishes will be fulfilled. Having a
tropical theme? Include a palm tree.

Etiquette pages now have questions such as: Is it proper
to have a color theme for a funeral? It is your funeral. If you
want to have a gentle white surrounding everyone, all white
flowers will set the tone. If you are more of a purple person,
specify just exactly how many irises you want. Flowers define
so much.

Bread feeds the body, indeed, but flowers feed also the soul.
> —Mohammad (c. 571–652), prophet of Islam

PROPS

The charm of fishing is that it is the pursuit of what is elusive but attainable, a perpetual series of occasions for hope.
—John Buchan (1875–1940), Scottish author
and politician

What do your fly fishing rod and hand-tied flies express about you? Props are becoming more and more popular at funeral services. A single item can say a great deal about you. You are "there" when people see a beautiful quilt you made, your toy poodle in the front row, your favorite hat, a shirt with your favorite team's logo, or a basket of flowers from your garden. Those who knew you will see these items and feel your presence as well. They are powerful tools and can be used extremely well.

PHOTOS—WORTH A THOUSAND WORDS

Photography does not create eternity, as art does; it embalms time.
—Andre Bazin (1918–1958), French film critic

Pictures are a wonderful tool for reminiscing. They are a glimpse of who you were at a particular time in your life, and where you were, and with whom you spent your time. Good photos capture your very essence.

You may take the time now to select particularly favorite photos of yourself to be used on a picture board. One consideration, however, is that collecting these photos can actually be very therapeutic for your family and friends when you are gone. These people need to participate in some aspects of your funeral plan. Perhaps consolidating old photos would be a cathartic exercise for them at this time. And even if you do hand pick all your favorite photos, there is no guarantee that they will not still include the one of you sopping wet, pulling yourself back into the boat.

CELEBRITY
EPITAPHS

TOGETHER
AGAIN.
-
GRACIE
ALLEN
AND
GEORGE
BURNS
(WRITTEN
TOGETHER)

A collection of photos can also be put together to form a video. There are businesses that now specialize in putting together video portraits, as they have come to be known. These folks will assemble your selected photos in any sequence you desire, and then put them to music. And, of course, you can choose the music as well. Another, more costly alternative, is to make a video starring you—as you. You can put together a staff to do a video about you, including an original script, professional actors, and animation for a mere $75,000. If this is your style, go for it.

A photograph is a most important document, and there is nothing more damning to go down to posterity than a silly, foolish smile caught and fixed forever.
—quoted by Elizabeth Wallace in *Mark Twain and the Happy Island*, 1913

PROGRAM

Whether people are gathered in a church, on a mountainside, or in a garden, a printed program makes them more comfortable. This agenda helps those present at the service to be more at ease, knowing the order of what is to come. At this point you will have made many personal decisions about elements of the service; this compilation leaves little question as to your wishes. The program may need to be tweaked somewhat depending on circumstances, but you can certainly create the bulk of it.

The program gives you another opportunity to include any thoughts you might want to share. These may be personal thoughts or quotations you have found meaningful. A short quotation says so much. What fun to be on the lookout for meaningful phrases to be left on a program encompassing your life.

You may choose your favorite photos for the front and back of the program. Selecting these all-important photos is another moment that can quickly put your life in perspective. Which photos are most important, why are they important, and what can be done to create more of these moments? Start taking more of those photos now.

IN LIEU OF ...

To give away money is an easy matter and any man's power. But to decide to whom to give it and how much and when, for what purpose and how, is neither in every man's power, nor an easy matter.
— Aristotle (384–322 B.C.), Greek critic, philosopher, physicist, and zoologist

> **Odd Deaths**
>
> **WILD BILL HICKOK**
> **1876**
> **Shot in the back of the head while playing poker.**

Another consideration is whether you want people to send flowers as a memorial to you, or have the money directed elsewhere. Donations can be made to various medical organizations, hospice, or a scholarship fund. Money may be directed toward a school, a library, or any worthwhile civic organization. If you have a passion, let the power of money support it after you are gone. The exercise of contemplating this choice defines some important priorities. On the other hand, if you want your loved ones to be surrounded by beautiful flowers, that's your choice.

INVITATIONS

If you are planning to have a memorial service, and if time permits, you may wish to see to one last detail. Perhaps you have always prided yourself on your unique invitations. Your funeral can be your last and most meaningful opportunity to create a final summons. Try to project yourself to that time when your friends and family will be gathering to celebrate your life. A spirited or thought-provoking quotation certainly could serve as an introduction. The time and place may be left blank, and you can leave a "guest list" for mailing. It also serves as an opportunity to acknowledge and thank all those who attend. The invitation can be very compelling.

A THANK YOU INVITATION

The question is not whether we will die, but how we will live.
—Joan Borysenko

A FINAL LIFE CELEBRATION

Time:
Place:

Please know that I have loved my life.
And what is to love in life but family and friends?
Therefore, I thank you from the bottom of my heart.

✿ ✿ ✿ ✿ ✿ ✿

JOIN ME FOR MY FINAL PARTY

It's not that I'm afraid to die, I just don't want to be there when it happens.
– Woody Allen

I WAS DYING TO BE HERE, BUT...

Time:
Place:

 That is the best—to laugh with someone because you think the same things are funny.
—Gloria Vanderbilt

Thanks everyone! I'll miss you—

Rules for a Jazz Funeral

Jazz funerals, most commonly found in New Orleans, have an etiquette all their own. A brass band leads the procession playing somber dirges and traditional hymns. After the body is buried and the procession moves away from the cemetery, the music becomes significantly more upbeat with people swaying and dancing. The family and close friends of the deceased make up the "first line" in the front. The "second line" is made up of those who were less familiar with the deceased, and even folks who are moved to join in the celebration. These people wave handkerchiefs and parasols as they follow along. The New Orleans jazz funeral celebrates the life of the deceased, while mourning the death.

READER,
IF CASH THOU ART
IN WANT OF ANY
DIG FIVE-FEET DEEP,
& YOU WILL FIND A PENNY

Mrs. Penny
(Graveyard unknown), England c. 1750

Here lies a man named Zeke
Second fastest draw in
Cripple Creek

–

Cripple Creek, Colorado

X.

AFTERPARTY

The informal gathering after the service is where the most healing takes place. People are one on one, sharing their stories and memories. Here is where tears and laughter are intermixed. So it is important that your presence be felt for the comfort it will bring as people share their feelings.

Many of the components previously suggested for your funeral service can be incorporated at this gathering. The formal service may be at a church, and the reception in a meadow. Having two segments allows you to express yourself in multiple ways.

YOUR FAVORITE FARE

A passage from *Being Dead Is No Excuse*, a novel about funerals in the Mississippi Delta, describes traditional reception menus in that area:

> "You can't bury a self-respecting Deltan without certain foods. Chief among these is tomato aspic with homemade mayonnaise—without which you practically can't get a death certificate—closely followed by Aunt Hebe's Coconut Cake, and Virginia's Butterbeans. 'You get the best food at funerals,' we always say, and it's true. Funeral procedure is something that we all just know. A legion of friends working behind the scenes, coordinating the food, makes sure the essential Delta death foods are represented in sufficient quantities."
>
> —From *Being Dead Is No Excuse*
> by Gayden Metcalfe and Charlotte Hays.

Lacking these ironclad traditions, you should plan and create your own personal menu. Pull out all the stops. Serve your favorite foods. Do you have favorite recipes? Ask someone to prepare and dish them up. Do you make your own wine? Put in a supply and have it served. Is the mushroom/pepperoni pizza from your local House of Pizza your favorite meal every Friday night? Plan for take-out. If you enjoy entertaining formally, arrange to have an event with white linens, silver, candles, your preferred delicacies, and a lovely wine. Your friends and family will most assuredly feel you there. People are identified with their culinary choices.

Bud loved to barbeque. He had a few favorite recipes that were all his own. Even his sauce had its own distinct smell. After Bud's service, everyone gathered in his backyard, cranked up the grill, and cooked up all his favorite dishes, even using the recipe for his own personal sauce. Bud was missed, but his presence was felt.

> ## Odd Deaths
>
> **FRANK HAYES**
> Jockey
> 1923
> He had a heart attack during a race. His horse, Sweet Kiss, won the race, making Hayes the only deceased jockey to win a race.

SETTING

Hold this event where people can sense your presence. Is there a particular beach or hiking trail that you especially love? Meet there and have a picnic. Were you the harbormaster for years and years? Gather on the dock around the boat. Perhaps an assembly at the bird sanctuary that you helped to preserve would be fitting. If your real joy was spending time with your friends at a local pub, by all means have folks gather there and feel your spirit. If you love to tinker and the garage is your second home, you might want to convene in the driveway. Just make the event yours!

When Tammy's grandmother died, the fitting memorial for her was clear. For years, each Sunday she had made her family one of her delicious dinners. At one o'clock the next Sunday afternoon, her family gathered at her home and ate dinner together. Each family made one of her celebrated dishes. The combined aromas captured her spirit as perhaps nothing else could. Even her silverware and dishes were reminiscent of her. Her home, her dishes, her food ... she was there.

MUSIC

Play your favorite music. Particularly if you held back and used more traditional music at your service, this is your opportunity to really do it! Ask that a jazz group play at this event. Or perhaps a great fiddler could infuse your spirit into the reception. Play chamber music. Put together a CD with your favorite tunes now. You can enjoy it and update it as time progresses. And it will be ready for your celebration.

Katie was a country music buff. If it twanged and rocked, she loved it! She was constantly putting together mixes of her current favorites. When folks gathered after her service, those collections were played. The sweet country tunes added a personal note for everyone.

KEEPSAKES

Perhaps akin to a "goodie bag," a small and meaningful keepsake can be a wonderful addition to this gathering. Just as buying a souvenir from a special place gives you a constant and pleasant memory of that time and place, so will a memento from this event. People will remember the camaraderie of the event, the inspirational feelings it evoked, and most importantly, you. It is probably best kept simple, but clearly one with meaning.

CELEBRITY
EPITAPHS

A TOMB NOW
SUFFICES FOR
HIM WHOM
THE WORLD
WAS NOT
ENOUGH
-
ALEXANDER
THE GREAT

Dave was an avid golfer. His wife, Maryann, gave each person at his service a gleaming new golf ball. She asked that each of them take the ball out on a beautiful sunny day, tee it up, and smack it off in memory of Dave.

Lenore loved beautiful shells, and combed the beach throughout her entire lifetime collecting unique conches, sand dollars, and periwinkles. She left a basket filled with her favorites and requested that each guest at her service take one as a remembrance.

The gathering after your service is really very important. Make yourself felt.

Odd Deaths

ANTON JOSEPH
CERMAK
Mayor of Chicago
1933
He was
assassinated by
accident while
riding
in a motorcade
with Franklin
Roosevelt.

ANNA HOPEWILL
Here lies the body of our Anna
Done to death by a banana
It wasn't the fruit
that laid her low
But the skin of the thing that
made her go

–

Enosburg Falls, Vermont

XI.

OBITUARIES

I wake up every morning at nine and grab for the morning paper.
Then I look at the obituary page. If my name is not on it, I get up.
—Benjamin Franklin (1706–1790), American
statesman, scientist, philosopher, printer,
writer, and inventor

You probably thought that the essay you wrote for your
college application was the most important one you would
ever write. That was a bit premature. The big one comes at
the end—your obituary.

Obituaries come in many sizes and styles. One may be the
simple facts delineating your life events. Another might be
a bit more personal and include lists of relatives. Some are
witty. Most important, however, an obituary should cover
the aspects of your life that matter most to you. Perhaps
you were an all-Star football player. While that is a major
accomplishment, perhaps the fact that you volunteered at
a local summer camp coaching children's football teams is
what you truly wish to be remembered for. And although
you might have headed a prestigious law firm that guided
some of the most esteemed financial institutions through
convoluted negotiations, your hand-tied flies could be what
you deem to be your greatest accomplishment. Your loved
ones will never know if you don't tell them.

Obituaries have become the focus of a new cult, as
witnessed by the formation of the Great Obituary Writers'
Conference. The annual conference attracts the authors
of these final tributes, as well as obituary junkies, who
are obsessed with reading them each day. Obituaries have
become a literary art form. It has been suggested that when
an accountant dies, his "number is up." Or innkeepers have
been described as "checking out." This brand of humor

might be described as a rather questionable attempt at putting the "fun" back into funerals.

Ideally, your obituary will have more substance than mere fodder for intellectual wit. A first-rate obituary will, with a nominal number of words, capture the spirit of your whole life. The likelihood of a random reporter, regardless of his abilities, divining your soul in a short article seems fairly remote. Time to put pen to paper, or fingers to keyboard, and compose your own obituary.

> *Bela Lugosi was buried in his Dracula costume.*

OBITUARY REALITIES

Obituaries appear routinely in large, prominent newspapers, in local daily newspapers, and in community weekly papers. A select, few people have an obituary appear in a large metropolitan newspaper. They are most often included due to the prestige of the subject, a quirk in the life of the deceased, or just plain old good timing. If you were a state senator, the last widow of a soldier from the Civil War, or gobbled up by a vagrant shark on a New Jersey beach, you are almost guaranteed a prominent obituary. Your chances are also improved if it is a slow news day without too many celebrities sharing the limelight. Lacking these criteria, however, you probably will not have a full-blown obituary in a major newspaper, but you are assured of being included in your smaller, regional paper.

Death notices are featured regularly in larger newspapers. These pieces are usually concise, and as a rule, merely factual, since they are rather expensive. An average abbreviated death notice in a metropolitan newspaper runs about $200 per day. This is not an occasion for verbose prose. Investigate your local papers and settle on a budget and content for your death notice and for your local obituary. It will not only be about you, but by you.

CONTENT

The brass tacks of obituaries are rather black and white. A quick perusal of obituaries in a reputable newspaper will give you those details. The essential facts concerning your relatives, educational accomplishments, occupational history, and special commendations generally are boilerplate. Date and cause of death will probably have to be provided by others.

The real heart of your obituary is yours to create. A good obituary will speak to each and every one of your accomplishments. A great obituary will reveal a small detail or vignette that captures your real inner-self. Perhaps you have been married to the same woman for more than fifty-two years. However, if you go on to say that you brought her a cup of tea in bed every morning, that reveals so much more. These are the facts that capture your essence.

The Portraits of Grief that were published by the *New York Times* after 9/11 are an excellent example of characterizing a personality in a few short words. A new form of obituary was a necessity after this terrible tragedy, as it seemed impossible to write traditional obituaries for the numerous victims. Jon Landman captured almost 1,600 individual people through his emblematic, usually endearing anecdotes, in his biographical mini-profiles. These abbreviated, yet inspiring obituaries, can spark your imagination and perhaps lead you to redefine your most important moments.

March 9, 2003

Mario Santoro: Good Food, Good Company

Yes, Mario Santoro was a dedicated emergency medical technician who loved his job. Yes, he doted on his daughter, Sofia, who is now 3. And yes, he was a passionate volunteer basketball coach at his local church who sometimes showed up to practice after catching only an hour or two of sleep, after a late shift on the job.

CELEBRITY EPITAPHS

GONE
BUT NOT
FORGOTTEN
-
CLYDE
BARROW

But those who knew him best also realized that Mr. Santoro, 28, loved, more than almost anything else, to have a great meal with close friends and family.

Steak. Seafood. Appetizers. Good wine, good beer. It almost didn't matter what was on the table, as long as the food was good and the company divine, said his widow, Léonor Ramos-Santoro.

"It was kind of like breathing for him; it was almost religious for him, like taking care of your soul," she said about her husband, who immigrated from Argentina as a young boy. "Meals were sacred. You sit down and you enjoy. You're not caught up in what's going on outside."

Sometimes the Santoros made their way to the Bridge Cafe, a restaurant not far from their apartment in Lower Manhattan. At home, Mr. Santoro relished his wife's arroz con gandules, or rice with pigeon peas, with an extra zing of garlic.

"For the rest of my life, I will want Mario to come home for a meal," she said. "If he has to go back, then fine, go back. But just one more meal, that's all."

—From *The New York Times* on the Web
© The New York Times Company,
Reprinted with Permission.

BENEFITS

If you sit down and begin writing your own obituary, it is almost guaranteed that you will gain an immeasurable perspective on your life. The composing in and of itself is cathartic. If you want an interesting and meaningful obituary, you will have to either employ some form of fiction or live an interesting and meaningful life. Bingo.

Imagine what it would be like to see your own obituary.

In 1888 a French newspaper wrote an obituary with the headline, "The Merchant of Death has Died." A fellow named Alfred was reading this article, which went on to describe how the deceased had invented dynamite, one of the world's most destructive forces. As it turned out, the obituary was written about the wrong man. The obituary was meant to be for Ludvig, Alfred's brother. Alfred himself was the man who had invented dynamite, and he was most distressed to see his life capsulated in this fashion. Alfred was an accomplished scientist with more than 350 other patents, who also wrote poetry and drama. As a pacifist, efforts to promote peace were of paramount importance to him. Alfred's surname was Nobel. He went on to establish and fund the Nobel Peace Prize. It has been suggested that reading this mistaken obituary was the impetus for his establishing this award.

Writing and previewing your own obituary can shed an interesting light on your life.

Odd Deaths

**HARRY
HOUDINI**
Magician
1926
He died of
a ruptured
appendix ...
on Halloween

Hollywood Cemetery, Richmond, Virginia

She drank good ale,
Good punch and wine
And lived to the age of 99

XII.

ETHICAL WILLS

What you have learned is as valuable as what you have earned.
—Susan B. Trumbull, founder of Personal Legacy
Advisors, LLC

A legal will is to your ethical will as a photo is to a painting. The photo depicts a scene in precise, accurate detail. A painting, however, is a more subjective and intuitive representation of the same scene. An ethical will bequeaths values rather than valuables. Rather than telling your loved ones what you are leaving them, it tells them what you want them to know.

LEGAL WILLS VERSUS ETHICAL WILLS

Clearly a legal will is a necessity. Increasingly, however, ethical wills are being recognized as equally valuable. This document imparts moral and religious values, lessons learned in life, and hopes and wishes for loved ones. An ethical will rises to a transcendent state.

Written ethical wills were in existence in medieval times and survive today with the same basic goal of passing on knowledge to future generations. They leave, in written form, those ideas and values to which you most closely ascribe. The goal is for you to leave a spiritual legacy to those left behind. Ideally, the ethical will serves as a window into your soul.

An ethical will works well in conjunction with your legal will, as it can both clarify and justify the logic behind decisions in the legal document. This document can also alleviate any confusion or misunderstandings by giving an explanation of potentially controversial components of your legal will. If money is being left to an organization or charity, it is valuable for the heirs to understand the motives behind this donation. Again, your values are the focus of these explanations.

UNSOLICITED ADVICE

If you have given sums of money to your heirs in your legal will, you might make use of your ethical will to dispense advice concerning its use. There are two fields of thought on including counsel. One assumes that the money is a gift and therefore may be used as the recipient sees fit. The other believes that the donor is entitled to clarify his or her wishes or hopes for the funds. Do you trust your heirs to remember and respect your zeal for assisting underprivileged students to attend your alma mater? Will they, in deference to you, donate funds to plant bulbs each spring around the Town Hall flagpole? Or do you hold their judgment in such high esteem that you entrust them with these assessments? Weigh your decisions carefully.

One must know not just how to accept a gift, but with what grace to share it.
—Maya Angelou, (1928–), American poet

FAMILY HISTORY

An ethical will can also describe your family's past history. It is a vehicle to transmit meaningful and important information from generation to generation. As people become increasingly mobile, the old family stories are being lost in verbal form. The sooner these stories are recorded permanently, the greater their chance of survival far into the future.

The personal events of your life, your accomplishments and disappointments, can be quite helpful to future generations. Select some of the most influential people in your life and detail how they affected you. Describe your greatest achievement, be it an award, a professional position, or a personal relationship. Advise those following you on dealing with disappointment. You have a lifetime of experience that has value to your heirs.

WRITING YOUR ETHICAL WILL

The length of your ethical will is your personal choice. The content may vary from two-and-a-half paragraphs to 250 pages. Try not to let excessive words dilute your content.

Some people have a difficult time getting started and find it easier to record their ethical will in video form. At some point, though, transcribe the content to written form as there is no guarantee that the future will include equipment to play a particular recording.

A mini-industry has sprung up to assist people in putting together their ethical wills. These companies will interview you and put together a great variety of finished products. There are also excellent books to help guide you through this exercise on your own. Try to write on acid-free or archival paper, as ideally this legacy will last for years to come.

Periodically update your ethical will as additional insights occur to you. You must also decide when to share this document with your loved ones. Oftentimes it is beneficial to present it to them before you die, as it is almost certain to evoke some meaningful discussions. Or it may be kept in a safe spot with other legal documents.

POTENTIAL DAMAGE

Another important aspect of an ethical will is to be aware of the potential damage any negative comments will have on your survivors. Once you are dead, you cannot retract anything you say. Is a slight from twenty years ago worth eradicating the worth of an entire lifetime? Is there real value in a final stab? Choose your words carefully and thoughtfully. These words are powerful.

CELEBRITY
EPITAPHS

A FRIEND
TO
HONESTY
AND A FOE
TO CRIME

–

ALLAN
PINKERTON

BENEFITS

Both a legal will and an ethical will impart a sense of control. Knowing that your affairs, both financially and spiritually, are in order gives a sense of peace and a feeling of closure. One assures that your worldly goods will be in the proper hands, and the other allows you to live on in the hearts and minds of your loved ones. Research has even shown that writing about emotionally significant and meaningful topics can be beneficial to your health.

The final value of writing an ethical will is the perspective it gives you on your present life and values. This reexamination of what you have learned in your lifetime, and the importance of certain values, forces you to confront yourself. If shared with others, it also compels you to "walk the talk" and potentially live a better life.

Dear Ben and Charlie,

Although I am in great shape, with no more adverse medical conditions than an occasional wounded knee when playing soccer, it occurs to me that time is passing and there are a few important issues I want to make clear. In a few years I will be retiring from commercial lobstering.

I know that each of you has other plans for your future and will not be pulling lobster traps from the sea. You have each made me proud in so many ways. I respect and admire all your choices.

As you know, my grandfather and father were both lobstermen and lived in our little house on the harbor. Although it appears that you will each be in the city pursuing your artistic and business endeavors, I hope that you will hold onto the house and use it in the summer as a family vacation house. Bring your children to swim, sail, and smell the fresh salt air. It pleases me to think of the house still being enjoyed by our family.

Love, Dad

*If they're willing to take my property, they should at least be willing
to consider my values.*
         —Rabbi Jack Rieme, writer, editor, and rabbi
            of Congregation Beth Tikvah,
            head of National Rabbinic Networker

Odd Deaths

MICHAEL
FINDLAY
Horror Film
Maker
1923
He was
decapitated by
a helicopter blade

Tomb of the Unknown Soldier

MARY JONES
Mary, Mary,
Quite contrary
How does your
Garden grow?
Quite well,
I bet,
Since it's well fed
By her body
Decomposing below

CONCLUSION

*It is a sad weakness, after all, that the thought of a man's death
hallows him anew to us; as if life were not sacred, too.*
— George Eliot (1819–1880), English novelist

You have made choices throughout your entire lifetime
that have defined your being, and your end is certainly no
time to leave things to chance. Your last chapter on earth
should reflect your personal dignity. At the final celebration
of your life, your very presence should saturate the room.
Ideally, those attending will leave having learned something
about living a fuller and more meaningful life through your
recollections and life choices. This event should be life
affirming for all your loved ones.

Ideally, planning your final life celebration will lead you on
a serendipitous journey that will give you a fresh perspective
on your life thus far. Is skiing down a mountaintop covered
in soft white powder your utopia? Or would you prefer
to be inert on a lounge chair sunk in white sands, sipping
something cool? Perhaps discovering a new species of birds in
a remote section of South Africa is your ideal. Have at it! Go
skiing, flop on a beach chair, or make a reservation on South
African Airlines. Be uncommonly diligent in embracing
those you love and having fun with them. It is imperative
to commemorate as many of life's events as possible. Be it a
birthday, an anniversary, a graduation, or a full moon, gather
those you love and celebrate with them!

Again, remember that your funeral is *about* you, but *for* the
living. If you have written your preferences for every little
detail for your funeral, that's great. However, if there are a few
things the folks left behind want to tweak to make them more
comfortable, you should make it clear that that is acceptable
to you. It will probably affect them more than you.

I am a big believer in planning my own birthday parties. I
don't like to leave those details to others. I know what I want
and I like to have it done just the way I want. Consider, for

instance, the man who carefully planned his wife's fiftieth birthday party. He called all her friends, made arrangements for a beautiful hall, ordered all the right food, and even arranged for a live band. At the last minute he called his wife's mother who lived out of town. She regretted that she had to decline, but observed that it certainly was going to be a surprise for her daughter because this was actually her forty-ninth birthday! Don't leave a once-in-a-lifetime event to chance—plan.

Each life ends with some sort of punctuation. Not terribly noteworthy is the common period. Been there, done it, the end. A question mark seems unfulfilling and perhaps a bit disappointing. Just what have I been doing all these years? The feelings surrounding an exclamation point seem like the winner to me. Yes! Fabulous! You go girl/boy! Very, very nice! Although maybe Gracie Allen had it right when she told George Burns that her life was going to end with a comma.

Do not fear death so much, but rather the inadequate life.
—Bertolt Brecht (1898–1956), German
communist dramatist, stage director,
and poet

PARABLE OF THE TWINS

Once upon a time, twin boys were conceived in the same womb. Weeks passed, and the twins developed. As their awareness grew, they laughed for joy: "Isn't it great that we were conceived? Isn't it great to be alive?"

Together the twins explored their world. When they found their mother's cord, which gave them life, they sang for joy: "How great is our mother's cord that she shares her own life with us?"

As weeks stretched into months, the twins noticed how much each was changing.

"What does it mean?" asked the one.

"It means that our stay in this world is drawing to an end," said the other one.

"But I don't want to go," said the one. "I want to stay here always."

"We have no choice," said the other one. "But maybe there is life after birth!"

"But how can there be?" responded the one. "We will shed our life cord, and how is life possible without it? Besides, we have seen evidence that others were here before us, and none of them have returned to tell us that there is life after birth. No, this is the end."

And so the one fell into deep despair, saying, "If conception ends in birth, what is the purpose of life in the womb? It's meaningless! Maybe there is no mother after all."

"But there has to be," protested the other. "How else did we get here? How do we remain alive?"

"Have you ever seen our mother?" said the one. "Maybe she lives only in our minds. Maybe we made her up because the idea made us feel good."

And so the last days in the womb were filled with deep questioning and fear. Finally, the moment of birth arrived.

When the twins had passed from their world, they opened their eyes and they cried. For what they saw exceeded their fondest dreams.

I put my wife beneath this stone
For her repose and for my own

–

Middlebury, Vermont

REFERENCES

BOOKS

Baum, Rachel R., ed. *Funeral and Memorial Service Readings, Poems and Tributes.* Jefferson, NC: McFarland and Company, Inc., 1999.

Carlson, Lisa. *Caring for Your Own Dead: Your Final Act of Love.* Hinesburg, VT: Upper Access Books, 1998.

Cochrane, Don S. *Simply Essential Funeral Planning Kit.* Bellingham, WA: Self-Counsel Press, 2002.

Copeland, Cyrus M., ed. *Farewell, Godspeed.* New York: Harmony Books, 2003.

Cromer, Michelle. *Exit Strategy.* New York, New York: Penguin Group, 2006.

Cross, David and Robert Bent. *Dead Ends.* New York: Penguin Group, 1991.

Grollman, Earl A. *Living When a Loved One Has Died.* Boston: Beacon Press, 1977.

Hogan, Pat. *Alison's Gift.* Silver Spring, MD: NOSILA Publishing, 1999.

James, Malcolm, and Victoria Lynn. *Last Wishes.* Valley Forge, PA: Mavami, Inc., 2000.

Kübler-Ross, Elisabeth. *On Death and Dying.* New York: Scribner, 1969.

Lamont, Corliss. *A Humanist Funeral Service.* Amherst, NY: Prometheus Books, 1954, 1977.

Llewellyn, John F. *Saying Goodbye Your Way.* Glendale, CA: Tropico Press, 2004.

Manning, Doug. *The Funeral.* Oklahoma City, OK: In-Sight Books, 2001.

Metcalfe, Gayden, and Charlotte Hays. *Being Dead Is No Excuse.* New York, NY: Miramax Books, 2005.

Moderow, Karen. *The Parting.* Alpharetta, GA: Jordan West Publications, 1996.

Pike, Robert E. *Laughter and Tears*. Eatontown, New Jersey: HH Press, 1971.

Power, Dale L. *Fancy Coffins to Make Yourself*. Atglen, PA: Schiffer Publishing Company, 2001.

Power, Dale L., and Jeffery B. Snyder. *Do-It-Yourself Tombstones & Other Markers*. Atglen, PA: Schiffer Publishing Company, 1999.

Schaeffer, Garry. *A Labor of Love*. San Diego, CA: GMS Publishing, 1998.

Seaburg, Carl, ed. *Great Occasions*. Boston: Skinner House Books, 1998.

Shushan, E.R. *Grave Matters*. New York: Ballantine Books, 1990.

Siegel, Marvin, ed. *The Last Word*. New York: William Morrow and Company, 1997.

Sublette, Kathleen, and Martin Flagg. *Final Celebrations*. Ventura, CA: Pathfinder Publisher of California, 1992.

Turnbull, Susan B. *The Wealth of Your Life*. Wenham, MA: Benedict Press, 2005.

Willson, Jane Wynne. *Funerals Without God*. Amherst, NY: Prometheus Books, 1990.

York, Sarah. *Remembering Well*. San Francisco, CA: Jossey-Bass, 2000.

VIDEOS

A Cemetery Special. Pittsburgh, PA: WQED Multimedia, 2005.

A Family Undertaking. Boston: Fanlight Productions.
www.pbs.org/pov/pofv2004/afamilyundertaking.

ONLINE REFERENCES

Alcor Life Extension Foundation
www.alcor.org

Baines, Barry K. *Ethical Wills*.
www.ethicalwill.com

Bates, Bill. *Life Appreciation Training*
www.lifeappreciation.com

Baxter, Denise. *The Blue Light Coffin Co*
www.bluelightcoffins.com

Ramp, Stefanie. "A Green Way of Dying." *Advocate Weekly* Newspapers,
1999.
www.newmassmedia.com/spring99/dying.html

Turnbull, Susan B. *The Wealth of Your Life*
www.yourethicalwill.com

Casket Furniture
www.casketfurniture.com

Casket Xpress
www.CasketXpress.com

Costco Funeral
www.Costco.com

Cremation Association of North America
www.cremationassociation.org

Crossings
www.crossings.org

Dictionary of Quotations
www.quotationsreference.com

Everlasting Memories, Inc.
www.evrmemories.com

Final Passages
www.finalpassages.org

Funeral Planning
www.funeralplan.com

Funerals: A Consumer Guide
www.ftc.gov/bcp/conline/pubs/services/funeral.htm

Glendale Memorial Nature Preserve
www.glendalenaturepreserve.org

Heaven on Earth
www.freespace.virgin.net/heaven.earth

Hollywood Forever Cemetery
www.hollywoodforevercemetery.com

130

In-Sight Books/Celebrants
www.insightbooks.com/Celebrants.aspx

International Order of the Golden Rule
www.ogr.org

Internet Cremation Society
www.cremation.org

Life Legacy Foundation
www.lifelegacy.org

Military Funeral Honors
www.militaryfuneralhonors.osd.mil/

National Funeral Directors Association
www.nfda.org

North House Folk School
www.northhouse.org

The Quotations Page
www.quotationspage.com

Quote Land
www.quoteland.com

Selected Independent Funeral Homes
www.selectedfuneralhomes.org

Space Services Incorporated
www.spaceservicesinc.com

Trappist Caskets
www.trappistcaskets.com

GUIDE FOR BOOK CLUB DISCUSSIONS

Here are some suggested topics to spark conversations among book groups.

These suggestions vary to accommodate groups that employ a strict literary analysis as well as those that discuss more personal responses. Enjoy—and rest assure—everyone has opinions on these topics.

1. Why do you think it is so difficult for people in our society to discuss death and funerals?

2. Consider both good and not-so-good funerals that you have attended. Discuss the differences.

3. How has this book changed your perspectives on funerals?

4. Have you ever had to organize a funeral "cold turkey" for a loved one? Was it difficult, and why?

5. How would you anticipate using this book? Is there one aspect that you would act upon sooner rather than later?

6. Discuss the pros and cons of sharing an ethical will with loved ones while you are still with them.

7. What particular vignette would you like someone to tell at your funeral? How does it define your spirit?

8. Discuss your obituary and describe what important details you would like included.

9. List your three most important successes and describe how you would creatively incorporate them into your funeral.

10. What aspect of your funeral do you think would be the most personal?

11. What are the most compelling reasons for planning your funeral?

12. When considering your personal regrets, do you feel it might be possible to rectify any situations now?

Here lies JOHNNY YEAST
Pardon me for not Rising

–

Ruidoso, New Mexico

PERSONAL FUNERAL PLANNER

Procrastination is the grave in which opportunity is buried.
—Unknown author

Now is the time to start jotting down notes and ideas you have for the funeral of your life. Record the first thoughts that enter your mind on these topics, as they may well be your most creative and unique ideas. You will probably notice as you compile these contemplations that a theme becomes evident. A formal person will start with engraved invitations and conclude with white linens. An outdoorsman will begin at the start of a trail and finish up with baked beans over an open fire. What are your thoughts and where will they take you? What fun to find out!

There are a myriad of details that should be left for your survivors. Many of these facts are rather boilerplate and may be delineated on forms specifically designed for this purpose. These forms are available from funeral homes, religious organizations, or even online. This is the responsible part of your funeral planning. The rest is the real gift.

These pages are meant to record your personal choices. Take some quiet time and give thoughtful consideration to each subject. Reflect on your preferences, priorities, and beliefs. Combined they have defined your life and will define your funeral as well. Poignant as they are, be sure to enjoy yourself as you go through this exercise, and take pleasure in your reflections. Not only is this notebook a meaningful and valuable resource for your survivors, it is also a wonderful tool for gaining perspectives for yourself. Enjoy.

FUNERAL HOMES

List at least three funeral homes you have visited.

_____

_____

_____

Consider the pros and cons of each funeral home and make a choice. Remember to consider Life Appreciation training when making this decision.

Funeral Home _____

Contact Information

_____

_____

Describe exactly what role you would like the funeral home and funeral director to play. Involvement from start to finish with prepayment is one end of the spectrum. Or you may pick and choose specific tasks for the funeral home and then delineate how you expect the remaining tasks to be carried out. Define a budget if you like. If you would rather not use a funeral home clarify your preference.

_____

_____

_____

_____

_____

_____

DISPOSITION OF THE BODY

Give a preference for burial or cremation.

☐ Burial
☐ Cremation

Define your choices concerning an open casket, closed casket, and embalming options

☐ Open Casket
☐ Closed Casket

Embalmment
☐ Yes
☐ No

Describe your casket preference. Choices are not limited so keep an open mind.

Preferred type of casket to be purchased

_____
_____
_____
_____
_____
_____
_____

Pre-purchased casket information

_____
_____
_____
_____

Address burial preferences.

☐ Underground

☐ Above ground in a mausoleum

If cremation is your choice, explain your thoughts concerning survivors being present at the cremation sight.

_____

_____

_____

_____

_____

_____

_____

Explain what you would like done with your ashes. They may be left in an urn or any special vessel of your choice. You may want to give thought as to whether you would like some or all of your ashes scattered in a favorite spot, in more than one spot, or any other personal choice. If you have chosen to be buried at sea, or blown up in fireworks, or wish to be left as a piece of jewelry, leave any information on these services that you might have gathered.

_____

_____

_____

_____

_____

_____

_____

_____

_____

_____

Let your survivors know if you wish to donate your body
or organs. Register with an organization to expedite this
process.

_____

Give thought to the importance of your survivor's need to
have a spot to come and "visit" you when you are gone. If
you have a preference for a marker at some spot other than a
cemetery, describe it.

_____

CEMETERIES

If appropriate, choose a cemetery. Consider the many pros
and cons of private, public, and even environmentally friendly
options. Investigate the financial stability of the cemetery. If
you are prepared, purchase a plot and record its location.
Record this information.

_____

_____

_____

_____

_____

_____

Choose a headstone, and clarify whether you would like
it to stand vertically or be flush with the ground. Define
size, material, shape and design. Or buy a headstone now and
have it engraved with appropriate information. Record this
information.

_____

_____

_____

_____

_____

_____

_____

_____

Write an epitaph. It may be fanciful, inspirational, witty, or just plain factual.

_____

_____

_____

_____

_____

_____

_____

_____

_____

_____

_____

TYPE OF SERVICE

Decide if you would like your service held in a church, and if so, which one. Also include the name of a particular clergyperson if you like. Weigh the importance of this location not only for yourself, but for your survivors as well.

_____

_____

_____

_____

_____

Record your preference for the location if it is other than a church.

_____

_____

_____

_____

_____

_____

_____

_____

_____

_____

_____

_____

Give careful consideration to using a Celebrant to officiate at your service. This alternative does not necessarily exclude a spiritual service, but it does open up many options for a more secular service. Explore and choose a particular celebrant if you wish.

Explore the Home Death option. While not for everyone, it is ideal for some. Make certain that the proper people are willing to be involved with this arrangement and list them.

FUNDAMENTALS

Locate and fill out a form with pertinent personal and financial information. Put it in a safe place, and tell at least two people where it is.

On a separate piece of paper, answer the personal assessment questions from Chapter VI. With the insights gained from this exercise in mind, write an outline for your service.

SERVICE BASICS

Write down readings you want included in your service.
You may also want to make a list of your preferred readers.

_____

_____

_____

_____

_____

_____

_____

_____

_____

_____

_____

_____

List musical selections you would like at your service. And
again, specify your wishes about people you might like to
perform these pieces.

_____

_____

_____

_____

_____

_____

_____

_____

_____

_____

_____

_____

Give some thought to your funeral procession. Include any thoughts you may have as to personalizing this part of the event.

_____

_____

_____

_____

_____

_____

_____

_____

_____

_____

_____

_____

_____

SERVICE ENHANCEMENTS

Write a Life Story Line. Detail life milestones in chronological order. Include interesting current events from your lifetime as well.

_____

_____

_____

_____

_____

_____

_____

_____

_____

_____

_____

_____

_____

_____

_____

_____

_____

_____

_____

_____

_____

_____

_____

_____

_____

Consider and list some of your personal memories. The unique facets of your everyday life oftentimes define you best. Include hobbies and recreational activities that are meaningful to you.

Describe some humorous events you have shared with others. Let your personal brand of humor shine through.

List the people you would like to participate in your service. If this list includes children, ask that they be given a choice as to whether they are comfortable joining in. Delegate these various tasks thoughtfully.

Consider what type of ceremony might make your presence felt. Ceremonies can be quite poignant.

List any traditions you might have that would be meaningful to incorporate.

_____

_____

_____

_____

_____

_____

_____

_____

_____

_____

_____

_____

_____

_____

_____

_____

_____

_____

_____

_____

_____

_____

_____

_____

_____

_____

_____

_____

_____

_____

SERVICE ACCESSORIES

Choose a location for your service. Make it personal.

_____

_____

_____

_____

_____

_____

_____

_____

_____

_____

_____

Describe what flowers that you prefer, and specify design and arrangements if you like.

_____

_____

_____

_____

_____

_____

_____

_____

_____

_____

_____

_____

Choose items from your life that were important to you that you would like displayed at your funeral. They will help to make your spirit felt.

_____
_____
_____
_____
_____
_____
_____
_____
_____
_____
_____
_____
_____

If you would like, put together a collection of significant photographs. Or, if you prefer, make a life video. You can create it yourself, or contact one of the many business set up for this task. Either leave these items with your personal information, or explain their location here.

_____
_____
_____
_____
_____
_____
_____
_____
_____

Another option is to design a program you would like used at your service. This may be left with your personal information, or describe its location here.

Create a personal invitation if you like. Leave it with a specified person to fill in the "blanks!" Again, this may be left with your personal information, or describe its location here.

Describe which causes, if any, you would like honored with donations in your memory.

AFTERPARY

List the details you prefer at either the party following
your service, or for the entire event. Include the time and
location.

Write a menu.

_____

_____

_____

_____

_____

_____

_____

_____

_____

_____

_____

_____

_____

_____

Consider the type of music you want to accompany the event. List the songs you might like played, or any live music you might like.

_____

_____

_____

_____

_____

_____

_____

_____

_____

Put together small keepsakes you might like given to the
attendees.

OBITUARIES

Consider the placement of your obituary. List appropriate newspapers and periodicals.

_____

_____

_____

_____

_____

_____

_____

_____

_____

_____

Write a concise death notice leaving the appropriate details blank.

_____

_____

_____

_____

_____

_____

_____

_____

_____

_____

_____

_____

_____

_____

_____

_____

_____

Write your obituary. Consider which life accomplishments you want to emphasize. You may want to include a personal vignette that you feel captures you spirit.

ETHICAL WILLS

Consider the value of an ethical will and, if you wish, write one. You may include a clarification of your legal will, a family history, or advice concerning any topics you like. Clarify at what point you want the ethical will to be shared. If might also be left with your personal information.

ABOUT THE AUTHOR

Betty Breuhaus loves a good party—a celebration of any event, be it a birthday, graduation, or a full moon. So what might appear as a preoccupation with death actually stems from her love of celebrations.

Recognizing that a funeral is indeed the final celebration of a life, she began a fascinating journey exploring styles, traditions, and options for funeral services. She began with innumerable hits on Amazon, hours of Googling, and extensive research in the library at Mt. Ida College, New England's foremost institution for funeral service education. Numerous interviews with funeral directors, ministers, and certified Celebrants followed. She also attended a Life Appreciation course for funeral directors led by Bill Bates, and earned a certified Celebrant certificate from a training led by Doug Manning of In-Sight Institute. Just sharing stories with family and friends turned out to be heartening and inspirational. The path had

an interesting tangent when she found that the planning process itself garnered great insights and fresh perspectives on life's great joys.

Betty Breuhaus lives with her family and dogs in Marblehead, Massachusetts.